fredericksburg 1862

"clear the way"

CARL SMITH

fredericksburg 1862

"clear the way"

Praeger Illustrated Military History Series

PRAEGER

Westport, Connecticut
London

Library of Congress Cataloging-in-Publication Data

Smith, Carl, 1946-
  Fredericksburg, 1862 : "Clear the way" / Carl Smith.
      p. cm. – (Praeger illustrated military history, ISSN 1547-206X)
  Originally published: Oxford: Osprey, 1999
  Includes bibliographical references and index.
  ISBN 0-275-98446-X (alk. paper)
  1. Fredericksburg, Battle of, Fredericksburg, Va., 1862. 2. Fredericksburg, Battle of,
  Fredericksburg, Va., 1862--Pictorial works. I. Title. II. Series.
  E474.85.S65   2004
  973.7'33–dc22   2004050375

British Library Cataloguing in Publication Data is available.

First published in paperback in 1999 by Osprey Publishing Limited, Elms Court,
Chapel Way, Botley, Oxford OX2 9LP. All rights reserved.

Copyright © 2004 by Osprey Publishing Limited

Library of Congress Catalog Card Number: 2004050375
ISBN: 0-275-98446-X
ISSN: 1547-206X

Praeger Publishers, 88 Post Road West, Westport, CT 06881
An imprint of Greenwood Publishing Group, Inc.
www.praeger.com

Printed in China through World Print Ltd.

The paper used in this book complies with the Permanent Paper Standard issued
by the National Information Standards Organization (Z39.48-1984).

10 9 8 7 6 5 4 3 2 1

FRONT COVER: *'Charge of Kimball's Brigade'*, Anne S. K. Brown Military Collection,
Brown University Library.

ILLUSTRATED BY: Adam Hook

CONTENTS

Key to military series symbols

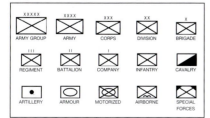

CAMPAIGN ORIGINS

Early winter in Virginia is changeable; variable warmth during the day and myriad water sources make fog a fact of life. Most days it burns off; many nights it lends the region an eerie graveyard chill; when the sky is leaden, no sun burns it off. Some days have a warm Indian summer quality, while others portend the frozen, bone-chilling days of February, when snowstorms can bring 18 inches in a day, wind-chill makes the eyes water and turns fingers into unresponsive lumps of flesh, and the humidity east of the Shenandoah drops wet, heavy snow that can snap the branches of cedar, oak, and maple. Most roads are unimproved, and rain or snow turns the rock-hard red mud into a slimy, gelled mass which clings to wheels and makes travel nearly impossible. Such a day was 7 November 1862, the first day of the Fredericksburg campaign.

This photograph, taken near Fredericksburg in winter 1862, shows a Union camp. Note the Sibley and squad tents as well as the scattering of partly melted snow which attests to the wide swings of temperature in Virginia.

The Army of the Potomac camped near Rectortown, outside Warrenton, soldiers huddled beneath blankets, looking like mounds of snow. Only orderlies, pickets, guards and duty officers stirred. Two officers arriving from Washington asked the officer of the day where the quarters of General Burnside and the commanding general were located. They were directed to a wind-ravaged tent where damp snow stuck to the canvas and piled in drifts against the walls. They carried two important messages – one for Burnside and one for McClellan.

Major General George B. McClellan's Army of the Potomac had beaten General Robert E. Lee on 17 September 1862 at Antietam, or so some claimed, but it had been a costly and imperfect Union victory, and the Confederate Army had escaped destruction. Lee had retreated from Antietam and his armies had moved out of Maryland and back into Virginia; the day had been saved by the molasses-like Union advance and the arrival of A. P. Hill. Even Burnside, who had been successful in a sea invasion of North Carolina, had been tardy in his advance across a bridgehead. Still, the costly engagement had stymied Lee's plan for a northern invasion.

McClellan pursued Lee at a leisurely pace. Perhaps organization was all McClellan could do, for he seemed reluctant to bring Lee into battle. On 3 October 1862, Lincoln wrote McClellan, asking, 'Are you not overcautious when you assume you cannot do what the enemy is constantly doing?'

Major General George B. McClellan and his wife, to whom he was devoted. This was taken prior to McClellan being relieved of command of the Army of the Potomac, in November 1862. Note his Napoleonesque pose.

Major General Ambrose Burnside, mounted, with his high crowned slouch hat and knee boots. An amiable man, he was chosen by Lincoln to succeed McClellan, possibly because Lincoln thought a friend of McClellan's would draw less criticism than another choice.

Lincoln was distressed, 'Give me a general who will fight with all his troops', he said. Then he turned his attention to finding a successor for McClellan.

In Virginia Lee's troops lay in a thin cordon around the massive Union line. Longstreet's corps was at Culpeper, south and southeast of Warrenton, and Jackson's corps was west, near Winchester in the Shenandoah Valley. Stuart's cavalry watched the fords south of the Army of the Potomac in case the Union became uncharacteristically active and swept down. At first Fredericksburg was unguarded.

The massive Army of the Potomac stretched from the western side of the Bull Run Mountains, near Manassas and Centerville, west to Warrenton, and still further west to Waterloo, New Baltimore, and Harper's Ferry. Bayard's cavalry patrolled along the front of the Federal line. In mid-November, unpredictable weather and the sluggish behavior of the Union troops led both sides to think about winter quarters.

One of the officers from Washington, General Catharinus P. Buckingham, went first to Burnside and presented his orders: assume command of the Army of the Potomac as soon as possible. Burnside protested that he was not the one who should command and that others were more qualified, but he felt he could not refuse presidential orders signed by the Secretary of War, Stanton. He accompanied Buckingham to see McClellan, made small talk briefly, and then handed him orders which relieved McClellan of command. McClellan stood silent a moment – relations with Lincoln were bad and he had been expecting this – then collected his thoughts and said, 'Well, Burnside, you are to command the army'. He knew Burnside's strengths and limitations and liked his affable subordinate, and although he thought Burnside responsible for much of the debacle at Antietam, he did not make it public knowledge; besides, they were friends.

Near Warrenton, Virginia, on 10 November 1862, soldiers cheered the retiring commander. George McClellan played to his audience, letting his immaculately groomed horse canter about. After McClellan's speech, the ceremonies dragged on. Burnside accepted formal command, and McClellan left the field amid cheers and kepi-waving, no doubt to meet with his political friends, who despised the way Lincoln was managing the war.

Burnside looked at his command and thought of Lincoln's advice to McClellan about aggressively attacking Lee. 'We should not so operate as to merely drive him [the enemy] away. As we must beat him somewhere, or fail finally, we can do it, if

at all, easier near to us than far away'. The letter continued, 'For a great part of the way you would be practically between the enemy and both Washington and Richmond, enabling us to spare you the greatest number of troops from here'. Clearly in Lincoln's eyes, McClellan's plans had been ineffective. If McClellan's slow, ponderous movements had been ineffective, perhaps a quick crossing of the Rappahannock and a strike on Richmond would be effective. Studying maps, Burnside noted that the closest area south of the Rappahannock to where he wanted to establish his supply base at Aquia Landing was a small town, one that was quaintly of another era, Fredericksburg.

Lincoln listened carefully and then conditionally approved Burnside's plan. On 14 November Halleck sent Burnside a terse note, saying, 'The President has assented to your plan. He thinks it will succeed if you move rapidly; otherwise not'.

Burnside had laid out a timetable and presented his plan for a cross-ing at Fredericksburg and headlong dash toward Richmond. He thought Halleck had understood and had agreed to his carefully devised time line, but Halleck and Burnside had miscommunicated, Halleck later asserted. After his conversation with Halleck, Burnside believed that the essential pontoon boats could arrive at Fredericksburg within days – probably three – as the Washington desk generals had predicted. Thus he began to plan, while the clock ticked. On 19 November 1862 Captain O. E. Hine of the 50th N. Y. Volunteers Engineers wrote to Brigadier General Daniel P. Woodbury, saying, 'I sent barge Three Brothers with 20 pontoon wagons to Belle Plain today... and... now another barge with 12 more pontoon wagons'. Things seemed to be going according to plan.

Burnside had reorganized the Army of the Potomac into Grand Divisions, and functionally, everyone was still learning how the new organization worked. Before reorganization, every corps commander would have reported to Burnside. Instead, Major General Edwin V. Sumner commanded the Right Grand Division, composed of I and VI Corps, Major General Joseph Hooker commanded the Center, com-posed of III and V Corps, and Major General William B. Franklin com-manded the Left, composed of II and IX Corps. Slocum's XII Corps was left at Harper's Ferry. Under the new structure, corps commanders reported to Grand Division commanders, who then reported to Burnside.

All three Grand Division commanders were older than Burnside. Sumner, the most loyal of the three, was an 'old army man' who had worn the uniform five years before Burnside's birth. Franklin was skeptical about Burnside's qualifications, and Hooker felt that he should have been given command himself, not Burnside. Although others in camp and in Washington felt that Hooker was better qualified, no one thought more so than Hooker himself. A political animal, he started off by giving Burnside less than his fullest co-operation and most sincere efforts, so not only did Burnside have to fight Lee and deal with Halleck's passive resistance, he had growing dissension in his ranks at the highest level.

Safe to say, as commander of the Army of the Potomac, Burnside had many rivers to cross.

Although disdained by McClellan, Abraham Lincoln was one of American's few presidents with only brief military service (in the Black Hawk War) who had a good grasp of military tactics and objectives. In the early war, a succession of inadequate commanders hampered Union plans.

General-in-Chief Henry Halleck was a political animal who hated his job and tried not to make controversial decisions. He opposed Burnside's plan for a Fredericksburg campaign, and favored McClellan's original suggestion, but Lincoln approved Burnside's plan of battle.

UNION COMMANDERS

Ambrose E. Burnside

A likable man, Burnside tried to do a good job but was a better subordinate than leader. He was aware of his limitations, and appears to have been honest in his personal assessment that others were better suited than he to command the Army of the Potomac.

Burnside was born on 23 May 1824 at Liberty, Indiana. Through his father's political connections he received an appointment to West Point, and he graduated in 1847 with the rank of 2nd lieutenant in the artillery. He served as a garrison commander in the Mexican-American War and in 1849 was wounded in a skirmish with Apaches. In 1853 he resigned his commission and started a company manufacturing breech-loading rifles which he had invented, but sadly the company failed. He was befriended by George McClellan and worked well with him on the Illinois Central railroad prior to the war.

At the start of the Civil War Burnside organized the 1st Rhode Island Infantry Volunteers and because Lincoln liked him, he was given responsibility for a naval assault on North Carolina. The assault was successful, providing a naval base of operations for the Union, and although somewhat minor in terms of military engagement, it was one of the first resounding Union 'victories'. Burnside was promoted to Major General of volunteers.

Major General Ambrose E. Burnside successfully conducted a naval landing in the Carolinas, invented a carbine, and developed huge side whiskers which are today known as sideburns – a play on his name. He is remembered mostly for the latter.

In July 1862 portions of his command were transferred to the Army of the Potomac (AOP) and Burnside was twice offered command of the AOP, but declined each time. At Antietam Burnside commanded both McClellan's former IX Corps and Hooker's I Corps, but he performed in a lackluster fashion, failing to seize the initiative at 'Burnside's Bridge'. As a result, McClellan privately felt that much of the blame for the Union loss at Antietam was caused by Burnside's poor performance.

Nevertheless, Lincoln was not happy with McClellan's performance and he approached Burnside a third time to ask him to assume command of the Army of the Potomac. This time Burnside accepted, possibly because he felt he was the best of the limited options available (another being Hooker, whom he felt would have been an unwise choice). Burnside's plan to take Fredericksburg and then move toward Richmond was a dismal failure. After repeatedly failing to carry Marye's Heights on 13 December 1862 and having his men suffer nearly 13,000 casualties, he wanted to lead an assault on the position the following day, perhaps hoping to die gloriously in battle and wipe out what he fig-

ured might have been a stain on his reputation. However, his subordinates talked him out of the final assault. Burnside then extended his resignation to Lincoln, but it was refused.

Burnside's subordinates did not give him their best, however, and Hooker led them in resisting his orders to the extent that after Fredericksburg, Burnside sought to have Hooker removed. This time when Burnside demanded that they be removed, Lincoln removed Franklin and Sumner – and Burnside, giving command of the AOP to Hooker, who would later show his true worth, at Chancellorsville.

Joseph (Fightin' Joe) Hooker

Born 13 November 1814 in Hadley, Massachusetts, Hooker attended West Point and graduated in 1837. Personally brave, Hooker was contentious and somewhat contemptuous of the abilities of others. He was given to intense self-promotion and denigrating the efforts of others. No one thought as highly of Joe Hooker as he did himself.

With the Civil War, Hooker was commissioned a Brigadier General in the volunteers and served with McClellan in the Peninsula in III Corps. Here, an ambitious newsman omitted a dash in an article about Hooker's activities. Hooker had replied to the question 'what are you doing?' with 'Fighting – Joe Hooker'. It appeared as 'Fightin' Joe Hooker', and the moniker stuck.

Hooker performed well at Second Manassas, Antietam, and at Fredericksburg, where he commanded the Center Grand Division. Still, he criticized Burnside loudly and frequently and was instrumental in getting Franklin to go to Washington to complain about Burnside. When Burnside sought to have Hooker removed from command and threatened to resign if Lincoln did not remove him, Chase may have intervened on Hooker's behalf and thus Burnside's offer of resignation was accepted and Hooker was made commander of the Army of the Potomac.

Fredericksburg was a sleepy little town, boasting three churches whose spires created its distinctive skyline. Taken in 1862 near Chatham (the Lacy House, Sumner's headquarters) this photo shows the town side, riverbank, and lack of bridges. Four months later, Barksdale and Sedgwick would fight over Marye's Heights again.

Edwin Vose Sumner

Edwin V. Sumner was the oldest active commander in the Civil War, having been born on 30 January 1797 in Boston, Massachusetts. Commissioned into the army, he lived to see one son-in-law fight for the South with Jackson and two become officers in the regular army at the outbreak of the war. Known by the nickname of 'Bull Head' Sumner, because of the supposed hardness of his skull – a spent musket ball had bounced off his head, he served in the peacetime army after the war of 1812 and in the Mexican-American War. Twice breveted, he was promoted to Lieutenant Colonel by the end of the war. He served with the 1st Cavalry, and when General David E. Twiggs resigned from Federal Service in 1861, Sumner was promoted as one of only three regular army Brigadier Generals.

Sumner was an 'old army' man and a soldier's soldier. He concerned himself with the job of commanding his corps, did not play politics, and supported his commanding officer, Burnside. Sumner was an active commander despite his advanced years, and his headquarters was always near the front, close to the action.

Sumner was given command of the Army of the Potomac's II Corps. Active in the Peninsular War with McClellan, he was twice wounded, and breveted to Major General for conduct at the Battle of Seven Pines. At Antietam he was criticized for leading men from the front rather than staying at the rear and 'conducting' his corps in battle. His headquarters was the Lacy House on the west river bank, overlooking the city.

William Buel Franklin

Born 27 February 1823 at York, Pennsylvania, Franklin graduated from West Point in 1843 at the top of his class. In the Topographical Engineers, Franklin surveyed the Great Lakes and took part in Phil Kearney's Rocky Mountains expedition. He was breveted for gallantry at Buena Vista during the Mexican-American War. Afterwards he was transferred to Washington, D.C. where he was responsible for the construction of the capital dome.

In 1861 he was a Colonel of the 12th US Infantry and fought at First Manassas. Afterwards he commanded a unit which was partly responsible for the defense of Washington. He commanded VI Corps in the Peninsular Campaign and at Antietam. When Burnside was appointed commander of the Army of the Potomac and reorganized it into Grand Divisions, Franklin was given command of the Left Grand Division.

He did not perform well at Fredericksburg, but part of the blame for this lies in ambiguous orders and directives given to him by Burnside, who later complained that much of the failure of the Union army at Fredericksburg was Franklin's fault. The fact is that for whatever reason, Franklin concerned himself more with securing and guarding the bridgeheads for retreat than knocking a hole in Jackson's line and rolling up the Confederate flank. Despite Burnside's accusations, President Lincoln refused to remove Franklin from the service but removed him from the Army of the Potomac when he relieved Burnside.

George Gordon Meade

George Meade was born on 31 December 1815 in Cadiz, Spain, where his father (an American) had supported Napoleon during the Napoleonic

Wars. He graduated from West Point in 1835 and resigned his commission in 1836. In 1842 he sought to gain re-appointment and became a 2nd Lieutenant in the Corps of Topographical Engineers. He served in the Mexican-American War, where he was breveted, and he was involved in surveying and geographical work from the end of that war until 1861.

At the insistence of Pennsylvania governor Curtin, Meade was made a Brigadier General of volunteers and given command of one of Pennsylvania's brigades. He served first in constructing defenses around Washington, D.C. and then with McClellan in the Peninsula. Wounded at Glendale, he led a brigade at Second Manassas and commanded a division in I Corps at Antietam.

At Fredericksburg Meade commanded the 3rd Division of John Reynolds' I Corps and was the commander responsible for the Union breakthrough into Jackson's line. Although initially successful, Meade's gains were not followed up quickly enough and the Union ground gained was lost in a Southern counterattack.

After Fredericksburg Meade commanded V Corps at Chancellorsville, where, after hearing of Hooker's decision to stop their advance, he impatiently demanded, 'If he can't hold the top of the hill, how can he hold the bottom?' After Hooker's failure at Chancellorsville, Meade was put in command of the Army of the Potomac three days prior to Gettysburg.

Thomas Francis Meagher

Born in Waterford, Ireland, 3 August 1823, Meagher was the son of a wealthy merchant. He quickly joined the ranks of Irishmen seeking independence from Great Britain and led an abortive movement in 1849 that could have ended in hanging but instead had him transported to a penal colony in Tasmania, from which he escaped. He made his way to the United States and traveled from the West Coast to New York, which had a large Irish population. Still, the seeds of Irish freedom were deep, and he became a familiar figure at rallies in the city.

In 1861 he founded a Zouave company that became a part of the 69th New York Militia under Michael Corcoran's command. As a major he led them at First Manassas. That winter he organized the Irish Brigade in

In winter 1862 the Union Army established a base camp at Aquia Landing (on Aquia Creek), which quickly blossomed into a bustling inland port during the Civil War.

12

General Robert E. Lee ordered Longstreet's Corps to Fredericksburg when the possibility of a Union attack became apparent; when he saw all that Burnside had gathered to oppose him, he ordered Jackson's Corps to come too. He is shown here on Traveller, his favorite horse.

New York City, and Lincoln appointed him Brigadier General of volunteers on 6 February 1862.

The Irish Brigade fought in every action from First Manassas to Chancellorsville. They carried a Federal flag and beside it the green standard with the golden Irish harp. Often they wore a spring of green in their forage caps to proudly denote that they were members of the Irish Brigade. It was at Fredericksburg, however, that this fighting unit stepped into the pages of legend, when they stormed Marye's Heights as part of Hancock's second wave attack and were the unit which came closest to the stone wall. Their fighting hearts led the Irish Brigade to bow their heads against shot and shell as if walking through a blizzard. Their dead lay in orderly ranks.

Afterwards the Irish Brigade was in dire need of replacements, but Meagher wanted no recruits; nor did he want the brigade disbanded and sent as replacements to other units. He viewed the brigade as a symbol of Irish freedom and determination, and so he resigned his command rather than see his beloved brigade sundered. His resignation was not accepted.

Winfield Scott Hancock

A twin, Winfield Scott Hancock was born 14 January 1824 near Norristown, Pennsylvania. He graduated from West Point in 1844 and served in the Indian Territory. In the Mexican-American War he was breveted for gallantry and afterwards served in actions against the Seminoles, against the Mormons, and as quartermaster for the US Army in Los Angeles.

Hancock established a reputation as a careful planner and a man of personal courage, who viewed the options and then acted on them, and also had great charm. His uniforms were always impeccable, and he never needlessly exposed his staff to danger. McClellan had him promoted to Brigadier General in September 1861, and he led a brigade in the Peninsular Campaign. At Antietam he assumed command of I Corps after its commander was wounded. At Fredericksburg he performed ably but was hampered by Burnside's orders, which limited initiative.

CONFEDERATE COMMANDERS

Robert E. Lee

Born into a historic Virginia family on 19 January 1807, Lee was related by marriage to George Washington. As a Lieutenant Colonel he led the US Marines, with J. E. B. Stuart's help, to quell John Brown's 1859 raid on Harper's Ferry. Although not a slave owner, Lee cast his lot with the South when the Civil War came because his ties to Virginia were stronger than his ties to the Federal government.

At first Lee was not given a large command, but his abilities rapidly became evident. He was appointed military advisor to President Jefferson Davis, and when Joseph E. Johnston was wounded at Seven

Pines, Lee assumed command of the Army of Northern Virginia.

Lee defeated Union armies at Seven Days Battles and Second Manassas, and then carried the war north in the 1862 Antietam Campaign. Although the 1862 Antietam Campaign was unsuccessful, Lee quickly re-established himself by not only meeting Burnside's thrust at Richmond, but setting a trap on Marye's Heights for the Union soldiers. After the victory at Fredericksburg, he defeated Hooker at Chancellorsville and then took the Confederate Army north for the Gettysburg Campaign.

Thomas J. (Stonewall) Jackson

Jackson was born in Clarksburg, Virginia (now West Virginia), 21 January 1824 and graduated from West Point in 1846. He served in the Mexican-American War and then accepted a teaching position at Virginia Military Institute (VMI) in 1852, resigning his commission.

At VMI he gained the reputation of being a teacher by rote, and many students called him 'Old Tom Fool.' At the beginning of the Civil War he was made a Colonel in the Virginia militia and sent to Harper's Ferry where he was shortly superseded by Joseph E. Johnston.

He acquired his nickname 'Stonewall' at First Manassas, when General Lee was trying to inspire and rally his men by pointing out Jackson, saying, 'There stands Jackson like a stone wall'. Shortly thereafter he was made Major General and sent to the Shenandoah Valley, where he fought three Union armies to a standstill. At Cross Keys and Port Republic his infantry gained the title of 'foot cavalry' for their rapid movement. He was one of two corps commanders in the Army of Northern Virginia.

At his best exercising independent command, Jackson did not perform in his normal fashion in the Seven Days Battles, but he redeemed himself with his magnificent showing at Second Manassas, Harper's Ferry, and Antietam where he is credited with saving the Army of Northern Virginia from annihilation by McClellan's troops.

He worked well with Lee, both seeming to share unspoken communication and understanding of events. Together they developed a relationship which allowed Jackson to exercise independent command while still helping the remainder of the Army of Northern Virginia stymie Union advances.

After Antietam Jackson followed Lee back to Virginia and stayed in the Shenandoah Valley more as a threat to the North than for any other military advantage. When Burnside moved toward Fredericksburg, Lee first sent Longstreet, and called on Jackson only when Burnside's plans became evident. At Fredericksburg Meade smashed through Lane and Archer in Jackson's line but was repulsed.

James Longstreet

Longstreet, the 'Old Warhorse' or 'Old Pete', as Lee called him, was born on 8 January 1821 in

General Thomas J. (Stonewall) Jackson was in the Shenandoah Valley when Lee sent for him to rejoin the Army of Northern Virginia at Fredericksburg because he feared a major Union offensive there and possible thrust at Richmond. Jackson arrived on 1 December.

Edgefield District, South Carolina. He graduated from West Point in 1842 and served in the Mexican-American War, being awarded two brevets for gallantry in action. He held the rank of Major when he resigned from the army in 1861, and four months later (October) he was made a Major General in the Confederate Army, and in October 1862 he was promoted to Lieutenant General. He distinguished himself in the Peninsular Campaign and at Second Manassas.

Although an able offensive commander, Longstreet's idea of the perfect battle was to be in a well fortified position and to have one's opponent smash itself to bits against his prepared position. At Fredericksburg units from his corps held Marye's Heights. Six waves of Union divisions broke on the ground in front of the stone wall, and Longstreet did not budge. Victory was complete.

Major General James Longstreet favored a defensive position, liking the idea of an enemy smashing himself against Confederate defenses. Most battles did not see Longstreet's men so well dug in, but he always thought that Fredericksburg was one of the South's high points in the war.

Thomas R. R. Cobb

Brigadier General Thomas Reade Rootes Cobb was born 10 April 1823 at Cherry Hill (a house) in Jefferson County, Georgia. Upon graduation from the University of Georgia, he became a lawyer, and compiled a new criminal code for the state of Georgia between 1858 and 1861.

When the Civil War started he was elected to the provisional Confederate Congress, from which he resigned to enter the Confederate Army. He recruited Cobb's Legion, a mixture of cavalry, infantry, and artillery which at first acted as an integral unit.

Cobb served in the Seven Days Battles, at Second Manassas, and in the Maryland Antietam campaign. He was promoted to Brigadier General on 1 November 1862.

He was with his unit, many of whom were also of Irish extraction, when the six Union waves struck the stone wall at Fredericksburg. He was killed in the second wave, when a musket ball hit his thigh (although some accounts claim it was shrapnel from an exploding shell which was fired at the Washington Artillery located just behind Cobb's position), severing a major blood vessel, and he bled to death while being transported to a nearby field hospital.

Maxcy Gregg

Born in Columbia, South Carolina, 1 August 1814, he attended South Carolina College and studied law. He was admitted to the bar in 1839. During the Mexican-American War he was an infantry Major, but he left to resume his law career when hostilities ceased. After South Carolina's secession Gregg was commissioned a Colonel in the 1st S. C. Infantry. In December 1861 he made Brigadier General. He served in the Peninsular Campaign, at Cedar Mountain, Second Manassas, and at Antietam, where he commanded a unit in A. P. Hill's Light Division.

His brigade was encamped directly behind Archer and Lane's positions on the Confederate right at Fredericksburg on 13 December when Meade's men attacked the line and buckled it. As Gregg's unit was to the rear of Lane and Archer, the men had their arms stacked and were unprepared for the Union attack. When the attack came Gregg ran forward to rally his troops and was mortally wounded. Carried to a nearby house, he died 15 December 1862.

THE UNION ARMY

The army of city boys was slowly changing, the green boys of '61 were veterans by late 1862, and men such as Reynolds, Meade, and Hancock had established themselves as capable and dependable commanders. Many of the pre-war weapons, uniforms, and armaments had gone as units were upgraded, and even the frock coat and Hardee hat were disappearing in favor of the kepi and sack coat. Most of the Mexican-American War vintage uniforms had been replaced.

In general, weapons were standardized, and some units exhibited esprit de corps such as the Iron Brigade, Excelsior Brigade, or the famous Irish Brigade, which was drawn primarily of Irishmen from New York, Massachusetts, and Pennsylvania. Many of these Irishmen fought for a cause they believed in – the rights of the individual under a law common to everyone. They fought because of their right of choice, some for the North, others for the South.

Two years of war and a seemingly endless string of commanders for the Army of the Potomac was taking its toll on morale. Even so, the army was no longer the mass of panicked ex-civilians which had nearly routed at First Manassas.

It was the Union leadership that had failed. Soldiers had wanted to pursue and bring the rebels to battle on ground of their choice. Burnside was generally well liked, and his success in the Carolinas gave them confidence in his abilities. The plan he proposed overall was sound. Still, there was dissension in the ranks: the bickering and jealousies of superior officers such as Hooker and Franklin were felt even at squad level.

Winter was coming, when traditionally armies did not campaign. Winter quarters would be good, and come the spring another offensive would put Lee in his place; besides, they had stopped the Confederate northern initiative.

Supply was second-rate. Some men did not have guns, and the commissary was often poorly stocked as war profiteers took advantage. The foot soldier paid the price in poor food, substandard clothing, and mediocre weapons. This again hurt morale.

Pay was sometimes in arrears, and some units were close to their dates for expiration of term of service and wanted to go home. This 90-day war had turned into a real conflict which was in its second year. The men were hardier, more fit, and experienced, but they lacked leadership. Still, they were willing to give Burnside a try.

The New York Light Artillery had several batteries in service at Fredericksburg. These men are officers in the regiment.
Note the variety of dress, from shell jackets and frock coats to light blue and regulation blue trousers.

The worst problem the Union army faced was that of command. Burnside turned down the role of commander twice before accepting it, and Hooker and Franklin both thought themselves more capable and better suited to command than Burnside. The greatest threat to the Army of the Potomac came not from without, but from within.

THE CONFEDERATE ARMY

Lee appeared to be finding his stride. Although smaller than the Army of the Potomac, the Army of Northern Virginia was a cohesive force. Jackson had shown how well he could operate under his own volition, and Lee was comfortable with letting him have his way as long as he stuck to the general plan. Longstreet and Stuart were able leaders who time and again had stood against superior numbers or had proven that training and experience would save the day.

Although supply was becoming an issue, as Lee mentioned in his summation of artillery pieces and numbers available to his corps commanders, the South was still generally well supplied. About this time reports began appearing of how much Union materiel had been salvaged from battlefields, including complete sets of equipment, racks of rifles, cases of ammunition, field pieces, and other salvageable uniform parts. These reports in the official records more clearly highlight Confederate materiel deficiencies than any reports which stated how low the Southerners were on supplies.

The year and a half of warfare had ravaged much of the farmlands in northern Virginia and the Shenandoah. Lee's army had to forage harder and further as crops were smaller. Some towns, such as Winchester, were occupied no less than 30 times during the war. Confederate weaponry was still eclectic, and the variety of weapons intensified throughout the remainder of the war. What good was it to capture several hundred breechloaders if you could only muster 30 rounds each for them? Many artillery batteries had four or more guns, often of three different bores. Although cavalry horses were still available, attrition was making the diminishing amount of re-mounts noticeable, even though the situation was not critical, it was serious and would only worsen as the war dragged on.

The average Confederate soldier was still superior to the average Union soldier, but the Yankees were closing the experience gap. Jackson's men prided themselves in their reputation as 'foot cavalry' who could move quickly and efficiently; in a landscape where roads were sometimes trails, railroads were often torn up, and mountains loomed everywhere, that was a skill to be reckoned with and appreciated.

Confederate soldiers, who were often country and farm boys, thought they were better soldiers than the average Union soldier who they regarded as softer city boys. Grudgingly they recognized that the Union troops were getting better. As soldiers they were often ill-disciplined in drill and ceremony but when the chips were down, they could fight ferociously – and they did.

CHRONOLOGY 1862

17 September – At Antietam the outnumbered, Army of Northern Virginia faces McClellan's advance. The ensuing battle is one of the bloodiest of the war, and the Corn Field, Bloody Lane, and Dunkard Church become household names. Federals have nearly 12,500 wounded, missing, and dead of 75,000, and the Confederates incur dead, wounded, and missing of around 13,500 of their 40,000 troops – nearly a third of their strength.

18 September – At night Lee withdraws across at Blackford's (or Boetler's) Ford.

19 September – Skirmishing occurs near Williamsport, Maryland. General Fitz John Porter crosses into Virginia in pursuit of Lee's army.

20 September – McClellan sends two divisions after Lee across the Potomac, but A. P. Hill's men confront them and they withdraw.

3 October – After having tallied McClellan's forces at about 88,000 effectives, Lincoln wryly calls them 'McClellan's bodyguard'.

6 October – Annoyed with McClellan's procrastination, Lincoln instructs Halleck to tell McClellan that he must 'cross the Potomac and give battle to the enemy or drive him south. Your army must move now while the roads are good'.

25 October – Lincoln shows his aggravation to McClellan, who has said that his horses are fatigued, by commenting in a telegram, 'Will you pardon me for asking what the horses of your army have done since the battle of Antietam that fatigue anything?'

26 October – The Army of the Potomac begins crossing into Virginia.

5 November – Lincoln orders McClellan removed as commander of the Army of the Potomac. Major General Burnside takes command of the army. At the same time Brigadier General Fitz John Porter is removed from command of V Corps and replaced by Hooker.

6 November – Both Longstreet and Jackson are promoted from Major General to Lieutenant General.

7 November – At Rectortown, Union officers arrive with orders relieving McClellan of command of the Army of the Potomac and putting Burnside in command.

9 November – Federal cavalry temporarily occupies Fredericksburg, Virginia.

10 November – McClellan says farewell to the Army of the Potomac in an official ceremony amid cheering by his soldiers.

14 November – Lincoln approves Burnside's plan to attack across the Rappahannock at Fredericksburg and drive on Richmond.

15 November – The Army of the Potomac starts moving toward Fredericksburg, from Warrenton.

17 November – Sumner's Right Grand Division arrives at Falmouth, across from Fredericksburg.

19 November – Longstreet's men occupy the heights above Fredericksburg while Burnside arrives at Falmouth and establishes his headquarters there.

20 November – General Lee arrives at Fredericksburg. Both armies escalate their concentrations at Fredericksburg. Jackson is still at Winchester but is planning to move.

21 November – Burnside has Sumner tell the citizens of Fredericksburg to surrender, but they refuse, so Burnside orders Sumner to bombard the town within 16 hours, which will give the citizens time to evacuate. Jackson begins moving toward Fredericksburg from Winchester.

22 November – Despite the time that has elapsed, Sumner opts not to bombard Fredericksburg as long as no 'hostile demonstration' on Union troops is made by either citizens or soldiers from within the town.

27 November – Burnside tells Lincoln of his intention to assault the Confederates massing on the heights behind the town. Lincoln favors a trefoil attack on the Confederates from sites along the Rappahannock and Pamunkey which will divide Lee's smaller army. Finally Lincoln tells Burnside he can conduct his frontal assault.

1 December – Union and Confederates troops skirmish at Beaver Dam Church and near Hartwood. Jackson's men begin taking up a position on the Confederate right, on the heights above Fredericksburg.

8 December – President of the Confederacy, Jefferson Davis, writes Lee that 'the disparity between our armies [in Mississippi and Tennessee] is so great as to fill me with apprehension'. He says it as a preface to denying Lee additional troops to defend Richmond.

10 December – Activity in the Army of the Potomac increases, telegraphing that a Union offensive is coming soon.

MOVE TOWARDS FREDERICKSBURG

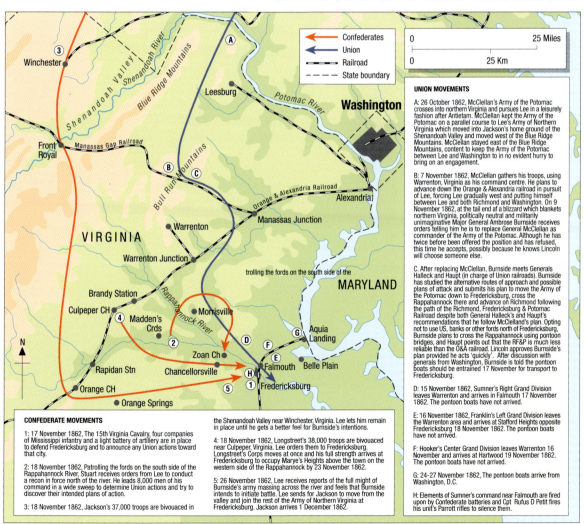

Confederates (red arrow)
Union (blue arrow)
Railroad
State boundary

0 — 25 Miles
0 — 25 Km

UNION MOVEMENTS

A: 26 October 1862, McClellan's Army of the Potomac crosses into northern Virginia and pursues Lee in a leisurely fashion after Antietam. McClellan kept the Army of the Potomac on a parallel course to Lee's Army of Northern Virginia which moved into Jackson's home ground of the Shenandoah Valley and moved west of the Blue Ridge Mountains. McClellan stayed east of the Blue Ridge Mountains, content to keep the Army of the Potomac between Lee and Washington to in no evident hurry to bring on an engagement.

B: 7 November 1862, McClellan gathers his troops, using Warrenton, Virginia as his command centre. He plans to advance down the Orange & Alexandria railroad in pursuit of Lee, forcing Lee gradually west and putting himself between Lee and both Richmond and Washington. On 9 November 1862, at the tail end af a blizzard which blankets northern Virginia, politically neutral and militarily unimaginative Major General Ambrose Burnside receives orders telling him he is to replace General McClellan as commander of the Army of the Potomac. Although he has twice before been offered the position and has refused, this time he accepts, possibly because he knows Lincoln will choose someone else.

C. After replacing McClellan, Burnside meets Generals Halleck and Haupt (in charge of Union railroads). Burnside has studied the alternative routes of approach and possible plans of attack and submits his plan to move the Army of the Potomac down to Fredericksburg, cross the Rappahannock there and advance on Richmond following the path of the Richmond, Fredericksburg & Potomac Railroad despite both General Halleck's and Haupt's recommendations that he follow McClelland's plan. Opting not to use US, banks or other fords north of Fredericksburg, Burnside plans to cross the Rappahannock using pontoon bridges, and Haupt points out that the RF&P is much less reliable than the O&A railroad. Lincoln approves Burnside's plan provided he acts 'quickly'. After discussion with generals from Washington, Burnside is told the pontoon boats should be entrained 17 November for transport to Fredericksburg.

D: 15 November 1862, Sumner's Right Grand Division leaves Warrenton and arrives in Falmouth 17 November 1862. The pontoon boats have not arrived.

E: 16 November 1862, Franklin's Left Grand Division leaves the Warrenton area and arrives at Stafford Heights opposite Fredericksburg 18 November 1862. The pontoon boats have not arrived.

F: Hooker's Center Grand Division leaves Warrenton 16 November and arrives at Hartwood 19 November 1862. The pontoon boats have not arrived.

G: 24-27 November 1862, The pontoon boats arrive from Washington, D.C.

H: Elements of Sumner's command near Falmouth are fired upon by Confederate batteries and Cpt Rufus D Petit fires his unit's Parrott rifles to silence them.

CONFEDERATE MOVEMENTS

1: 17 November 1862, The 15th Virginia Cavalry, four companies of Mississippi infantry and a light battery of artillery are in place to defend Fredericksburg and to announce any Union actions toward that city.

2: 18 November 1862, Patrolling the fords on the south side of the Rappahannock River, Stuart receives orders from Lee to conduct a recon in force north of the river. He leads 8,000 men of his command in a wide sweep to determine Union actions and try to discover their intended plans of action.

3: 18 November 1862, Jackson's 37,000 troops are bivouaced in the Shenandoah Valley near Winchester, Virginia. Lee lets him remain in place until he gets a better feel for Burnside's intentions.

4: 18 November 1862, Longstreet's 38,000 troops are bivouaced near Culpeper, Virginia. Lee orders them to Fredericksburg. Longstreet's Corps moves at once and his full strength arrives at Fredericksburg to occupy Marye's Heights above the town on the western side of the Rappahannock by 23 November 1862.

5: 26 November 1862, Lee receives reports of the full might of Burnside's army massing across the river and feels that Burnside intends to initiate battle. Lee sends for Jackson to move from the valley and join the rest of the Army of Northern Virginia at Fredericksburg. Jackson arrives 1 December 1862.

BURNSIDE'S APPROACH

As soon as Lincoln approved his plan, Burnside put the Army of the Potomac in motion – no one would accuse him of failing to move quickly. The army marched for Fredericksburg in three segments, one for each Grand Division, careful to appear to move toward Aquia Creek, where Lee might assume they were heading for winter quarters. Lee might then disperse the Army of Northern Virginia to winter quarters and leave Burnside fewer Southern troops to contend with.

Lee was cautious. When he had heard of Burnside's promotion, he had been concerned because the genial general was an unknown quantity. He had even made a small joke to Longstreet about how sad he was to see McClellan replaced, because he 'understood' McClellan so well. Burnside, however, was apt to be more aggressive, and that might mean he would try something unexpected.

Fredericksburg lies at a bend just below the junction of the Rappahannock and Rapidan rivers. Before the American Revolution, it was a commercial center, with its riverside setting and mills; upstream a dam near Falmouth regulated the flow of water, which attracted mill owners. A canal extended from the bend of the river to the northern end of Charles and Princess Anne streets, where it collected in a pool. A mill-race bordered the north end of town.

The town runs north-south on a plain on the western side of the river, and on the eastern shore Stafford Heights rise sharply from the river-bank to dominate Fredericksburg. The city itself sits on a raised plain so anyone approaching from the river is hidden from view by the bank once they are half-way across. A mile west of town Telegraph Road follows a string of hills south from Marye's Heights, over Howison, Willis, and Prospect Hills, which rise above the town and its southern approaches. Although Marye's Heights dominate the town, artillery there could not control the higher Stafford Heights across the river, as the distance and difference in heights are too great. An enemy controlling the town but not Marye's Heights would forever be at the mercy of gun emplacements in the hills.

The Old Richmond Stage Road runs south from Fredericksburg; a quarter mile from the river; the Richmond, Fredericksburg and Potomac (RF&P) Railroad follows the old stage road a quarter of a mile further away. The bridge from Fredericksburg east was destroyed early in the war. Prospect Hill touches on Deep Run, a natural watercourse and obstacle south of the city,

These men from Maine were in one of the waves charging Marye's Heights in December 1862. Their kepis seem to bear a clover, symbol of II Corps, Army of the Potomac. They are probably from the 19th Maine.

The vast number of supply wagons for the Army of the Potomac show why a quiet approach to the bridgeheads was probably unrealistic. Even an untrained observer would know something was happening when he saw this many wagons.

Union soldiers on the march, following their rather grown-up looking drummer. Note they march with fixed sword bayonets. Formations like this advanced through town attracting Confederate artillery fire, before going into a line and advancing up Marye's Heights into the guns of the waiting Confederates.

above Hamilton's Crossing, where roads intersect south of town and Deep Run, but north of the Massaponax River which flows east-west.

The Confederates secretly extended Telegraph Road into a military road which reached to Marye's Heights, running along the elevation slightly below the ridge-line, making it difficult to see until you were almost upon it. A stone wall along Marye's Heights concealed this new 'sunken' road. North of the sunken road a line of rifle pits was dug before Burnside assaulted the heights, and these would reach the woods. All considered, Marye's Heights, with the stone wall, was a natural firing parapet with a slight salient. Fifty yards east of the stone wall ran a wooden fence to discourage animals from straying. Closer to town a slight depression broke the gradual rise from the city to the stone wall. The mill race had stringers crossing it but no planks.

Burnside planned to advance to Aquia Landing, then dash for Fredericksburg, throw pontoon bridges across, and be in Richmond before Lee could stop him. It was a decidedly different approach to the methodical plodding of McClellan, but so much depended upon timing. As Lincoln had cautioned when approving the plan, with speed it would succeed, otherwise, not.

Finally, officers assured Burnside the boats would be entrained by 17 November 1862, so he planned for his troops to converge on the area about the time the pontoon boats would arrive, thus keeping the element of surprise. On 15 November General Sumner's Right Grand Division of 37,432 men left Warrenton, heading in the general direction of Aquia Creek, the newly built supply depot. They arrived in Falmouth, not far from Fredericksburg, on 17 November. On 16 November, General W. B. Franklin's Left Grand Division of 53,543 troops had marched away from the Warrenton area and they arrived two days later at Stafford Heights. There was no sign of the pontoon boats and Burnside was understandably concerned, sensing that the element of surprise was slipping away.

Unknown to Burnside, Lee was cautious and sent a small force consisting of the 15th Virginia Cavalry, four companies of Mississippi infantry, and a light artillery battery to garrison Fredericksburg and relay word of Union activities near the city. Events were rapidly coming to a head, and on 18 November, while patrolling fords south of the Rappahannock, Stuart received orders to take his 8,000 troopers and conduct a recon in force north of the river. That same day Lee ordered Longstreet's 38,000 men, who were bivouacked near Culpeper, to head toward Fredericksburg. Longstreet moved immediately. Lee allowed Jackson's 37,000 men to remain in the valley near Winchester as a possible deterrent. Lee probably did not guess Burnside's intentions until later, but as an astute commander, he would not remain in place and allow his adversary to maneuver at will.

Hooker's Center Grand Division of 47,952 soldiers left Warrenton on 16 November and arrived at Hartwood Church on 19 November. Still no pontoon boats had arrived, yet the army of nearly 150,000 massed, awaiting orders. By this time, Lee had heard from scouts and friendly civilians of Union activity east of the river, but because Burnside had not moved closer to town, Lee waited and allowed Jackson to remain in the valley, foraging.

On 23 November Longstreet's corps of 38,320 men arrived to occupy Marye's Heights. Lee still did not know for certain what Burnside planned. Finally, on 24 November, the pontoon boats began to arrive. On 26 November Lee received reports that Burnside was massing the Army of the Potomac for what appeared to be an attack on Fredericksburg, and he sent orders to Jackson to rejoin the Army of Northern Virginia at Fredericksburg.

By 27 November all pontoon boats were gathered near Fredericksburg. Confederate batteries fired on elements of General Sumner's corps near Falmouth. Captain Rufus D. Petit fired his Parrott rifles in response to the Confederate salvo. When he learned of it, Burnside was concerned that this counter-battery fire might somehow have betrayed his intentions to Lee.

Burnside chose three sites to cross, all in areas where ruined bridges or fords were located. On his side of the river Stafford Heights fall sharply to the water's edge – hardly the ideal spot for moving cumbersome wagons downhill in preparation for anchoring pontoon boats to build bridges. Wagons were noisy, but the mules pulling them were noisier still, as was the laying of bridges. Still, speed was of the essence, and it was only when army engineers and teamsters arrived that they realized they were under the inquiring eyes of Confederates, who now occupied the city. To be precise, the Upper and Middle Crossings were right in view of Confederate pickets. No doubt Burnside felt the possibility of surprise fade with the disappearance of the morning fog.

Jackson's corps of 36,087 troops arrived on 1 December. Combined with Stuart's command of 10,016 troopers and Pendleton's 792 reserve artillerists, Burnside had nearly twice as many men as Lee, but Lee held Marye's Heights.

Burnside had everything he needed at Fredericksburg by 19 November, except pontoon boats to lay the bridges on. While he awaited the arrival of the boats, initiative and the element of surprise dribbled away.

FREDERICKSBURG ORDER OF BATTLE

Alabama = Ala.; Arkansas = Ark.; Connecticut = Conn.; Delaware = Del.; Florida = Fla.; Georgia =Ga.; Illinois = Ill.; Indiana = Ind.; Louisiana = La.; Maryland = Md.; Massachusetts = Mass.; Michigan = Mich.; Minnesota = Minn.; Mississippi = Miss.; New Hampshire = N. H.; New Jersey = N. J.; New York = N. Y.; North Carolina = N. C.; Pennsylvania = Penn.; Rhode Island = R. I.; South Carolina = S. C.; Tennessee = Tenn.; Virginia = Va.; Wisconsin = Wisc.; Brig.Gen. = Brigadier General; Col. = Colonel; Lt.Col. = Lieutenant Colonel; Maj. = Major; Cpt. = Captain; 1st Lt. = 1st Lieutenant; 2nd Lt. = 2nd Lieutenant. Numbers in parentheses are the amount of troops present; when numbers are extrapolated, 'c.' appears in front of them. Artillery units have the number of guns with a slash (/) separating the kinds of guns. Gun abbreviations are: 12N = 12lb. Napoleon gun; 6SB = 6lb. smooth bore; 10P = 10lb. Parrott rifle; 20P = 20lb. Parrott rifle; W = Whitworth gun; JR = James rifle; HR = Hotchkiss rifle; BR = Blakely rifle; 3R = 3-inch rifle; 3.5R = 3 1/2 inch rifle; 4.5R = 4 1/2-inch rifle; 12H = 12lb. howitzer; 24H = 24lb. howitzer.

ARMY OF THE POTOMAC

Maj.Gen. Ambrose E. Burnside
Reported strength of soldiers available: 142,551
Staff: (28)

VOLUNTEER ENGINEER BRIGADE
Brig.Gen. Daniel P. Woodbury (c.1,540)
15th N. Y. Engineers – James A. Magruder combined with
50th N. Y. Engineers – Ira Spaulding (c.1,107)
US Regular Engineer Battalion – 1st Lt. Charles E. Cross (c.433)

SIGNAL CORPS
Cpt. S.T. Cushing (171)

QUARTERMASTER GUARD
Lt.Col. Rufus Ingalls (343)

ESCORT (C.142)
Oneida Cavalry – Cpt. Daniel P. Mann (64)
1st US Cavalry (detachment) – Maj. Marcus A. Reno (c.28)
A&E/4th US Cavalry – Cpt. James B. McIntyre (c.50)

PROVOST GUARD
Brig.Gen. Marsena Patrick (5,239)
A/McClellan Ill. Dragoons – Cpt. George W. Shears (c.37)
B/McClellan Ill. Dragoons – Cpt. David C. Brown (c.35)
2nd US Cavalry – Maj. Charles J. Whiting/Cpt. Theopilius F. Rodenbough (c.443)
G/9th N. Y. – Cpt. Charles Child (c.43)
93rd N. Y. – Col. John S. Crocker (c.310)
8th US Infantry – Cpt. Royal T. Frank (c.464)

ARTILLERY

Brig.Gen. Henry J. Hunt

ARTILLERY RESERVE
Lt.Col. William Hays (c.1,360) Staff: 4
A/1st N. Y. Lt. Bttn. – Cpt. Otto Dietrichs (c.154) 4/20lb.
B/1st N. Y. Lt. Bttn. – Cpt. Adolph Voegelee (173) 4/20lb.
C/1st N. Y. Lt. Bttn. – 1st Lt. Bernhard Wever (98) 4/10lb.
D/1st N. Y. Lt. Bttn. – Cpt. Chas. Kusserow (134) 6/3R
5th N. Y. Light Btty. – Cpt. Elijah D. Taft (c.146) 4/20lb.
K/1st US Arty. – Cpt. Wm. M. Graham (73) 6/12lb.
A/2nd US Arty. – Cpt. John C. Tidball (c.75) 6/3R

G/4th US Arty. – 1st Lt. Marcus P. Miller (c.122) 4/12lb.
K/5th US Arty. – 1st Lt. David H. Kinzie (c.114) 4/12lb.

ARTILLERY TRAIN GUARD
C/32nd Mass. – Cpt. Josiah C. Fuller (c.48)

UNATTACHED
Maj. Thomas S. Trumbull (c.219)
B/1st Conn. Heavy Arty. – Cpt. Albert F. Booker (c.109) 4/4.5 guns
M/1st Conn. Heavy Arty. – Cpt. Franklin A. Pratt (c.110) 3/4.5 guns

LEFT GRAND DIVISION

Maj.Gen. Wm. B. Franklin
Reported strength: 53,543

ESCORT
6th Penn. cavalry – Col. Richard H. Rush (Rush's Lancers) (c.244)

I CORPS

Brig.Gen. John F. Reynolds (c.16,484)

ESCORT
L/1st Maine Cavalry – Cpt. Constantine Taylor (c.32)

1ST DIVISION

Brig.Gen. Abner Doubleday (c.5,533)

1ST BRIGADE
Col. Walter Phelps Jr. (c.1,299) Staff: 15
2nd US Sharpshooters – Maj. Homer R. Stoughton (198)
84th (14th Militia) N. Y. – Lt.Col. William H. de Bevoise (c.42)
22nd N. Y. – Lt.Col. J. McKee Jr. (c.305)
24th N. Y. – Col. Samuel R. Beardsley/Maj. R. Oliver Jr. (c.301)
30th N. Y. – Lt.Col. Morgan H. Chrysler (c.438)

2ND BRIGADE
Col. James Gavin (c.1349) Staff: 8
56th Penn. – Lt.Col. William Hoffman (c.262)
76th N. Y. – Col. William P. Wainwright (c.378)
95th N. Y. – Col. George H. Biddle/Lt.Col. J. B. Post (c.263)
7th Ind. – Lt.Col. John F. Cheek (c.438)

3RD BRIGADE
Brig.Gen. Gabriel R. Paul/Col. William F. Rogers (c.1,306) Staff: 3
80th N. Y. – Lt.Col. Jacob B. Hardenbergh (348)
21st N. Y. – Cpt. George N. Layton (c.79)
23rd N. Y. – Col. Henry C. Hoffman (c.521)
35th N. Y. – Col. Newton B. Lord (355)

4TH BRIGADE (IRON BDE.)
Brig.Gen. Solomon Meredith/Col. Lysander Cutler (c.1,230) Staff: 2
2nd Wisc. – Col. Lucius Fairchild (c.228)
6th Wisc. – Lt.Col. Edw. S. Bragg (c.162)
7th Wisc. – Col. Wm. W. Robinson (Lt.Col. C. A. Hamilton) (c.152)
19th Ind. – Lt.Col. Samuel J. Williams (c.174)
24th Mich. – Col. Henry A. Morrow (c.512)

In winter 1862 Union cavalry was attached to a Grand Division. It was used for provost duty, recon, and carrying messages, but was of little real offensive use and saw little action, prompting many infantrymen to mutter, 'I never saw a dead cavalryman'.

1ST DIVISION ARTILLERY
Cpt. G. A. Gerrish/Cpt. John A. Reynolds (*c.*349)
B/4th US Arty – 1st Lt. James Stewart (*c.*129) 6/12N
A/1st N. H. – 1st Lt. Frederick M. Edgell (*c.*85) 4/3R
L/1st N. Y. Lt. Arty – Cpt. John A. Reynolds (135) 4/3R

2ND DIVISION

Brig.Gen. John Gibbon/Brig.Gen. Nelson Taylor (*c.*5,029) Staff: 6

1ST BRIGADE
Col. Adrian R. Root (*c.*1,639) Staff: 4
94th N. Y. – Maj. John A. Kress (519)
104th N. Y. – Maj. Gilbert G. Prey (*c.*324)
105th N. Y. – Maj. Daniel A. Sharp/Cpt. Abraham Moore (177)
107th Penn. – Col. Thomas F. McCoy (188)
16th Maine – Lt.Col. Chas.W. Tilden (427)

2ND BRIGADE
Col. Peter Lyle (*c.*1,347) Staff: 4
26th N. Y. – Lt.Col. Gilbert S. Jennings/Maj. Ezra Wetmore (300)
12th Mass. – Col. James L. Bates (258)
90th Penn. – Lt.Col. Wm. A. Leech (*c.*241)
136th Penn. – Col. Thomas M. Bayne (*c.*544)

3RD BRIGADE
Brig.Gen. Nelson Taylor/ Col. Samuel S. Leonard (*c.*1,576) Staff: 11
83rd N. Y. – Cpt. John Hendrickson (292)
97th N. Y. – Col. Charles Wheelock (278)
13th Mass. – Col. Samuel H. Leonard/Lt.Col. Walter Batchelder (*c.*307)
11th Penn. – Col. Richard Coulter (394)
88th Penn. – Col. G. P. McLean (Maj. David A. Griffith) (*c.*294)

2ND DIVISION ARTILLERY
Cpt. George. F. Leppien (*c.*461)
F/1st Penn. Lt. Arty – 1st Lt. R. Bruce Ricketts (*c.*105) 4/3R

C/Penn. Light Arty – Cpt. James Thompson (*c.*109) 4/3R
5th Maine Arty Blly. – Cpt. Geo. F. Lieppen (*c.*118) 6/12N
2nd Maine Arty Btty. – Cpt. James A. Hall (*c.*129) 6/3R

3RD DIVISION

Maj.Gen. George G. Meade (*c.*5,890) Staff: 7

1ST BRIGADE
Col. William Sinclair/Col. Wm. McCandless (*c.*1,609) Staff: 4
1st Rifles – Cpt. Charles F. Taylor (*c.*289)
1st Penn. Reserves – Cpt. W. C. Talley (389)
2nd Penn. Reserves – Col. W. McCandless/Cpt. Timothy Mealey (244)
6th Penn. Reserves – Maj. Wellington H. Ent (377)
121st Penn. – Col. Chapman Biddle (*c.*306)

2ND BRIGADE
Col. Albert L. Magilton (1962) Staff: 2
3rd Penn. Reserves – Col. Horatio G. Sickel (452)
4th Penn. Reserves – Lt.Col. Richard H. Woolworth (349)
7th Penn. Reserves – Col. Henry C. Bolinger (345)
8th Penn. Reserves – Maj. Silas M. Bailey (264)
142nd Penn. – Col. Robert P. Cummins (550)

3RD BRIGADE
Brig.Gen. C. Feger Jackson (1744) Staff: 3
5th Penn. Reserves – Col. J. W. Fisher/Lt.Col. George Dare (322)
9th Penn. Reserves – Lt.Col. Robert Anderson /Maj. James M. Snodgrass (401)
10th Penn. Reserves – Lt.Col. A. J. Warner (Maj. James B. Knox) (401)

11th Penn. Reserves – Lt.Col. Samuel M. Jackson (208)
12th Penn. Reserves – Cpt. Richard Gustin (329)

3RD DIVISION ARTILLERY (*c.*499)
A/1st Penn. Light – 1st Lt. John G. Simpson (*c.*102) 4/12N
B/1st Penn. Light – Cpt. James H. Cooper (*c.*108) 4/3R
G/1st Penn. Light – Cpt. Frank P. Amsden (*c.*160) 4/3R
C/5th US Arty – Cpt. Dunbar R. Ranson (*c.*129) 4/12N

EXTRA CAISSONS
F/2nd Penn. Reserves – Cpt. J. M. Clark (*c.*69)

VI CORPS

Maj.Gen. William F. Smith (*c.*24,230) Staff: 13

ESCORT
10th N. Y. Cavalry – 1st Lt. George Vanderbilt (*c.*333)
I/6th Penn. Cavalry – Cpt. James Starr (*c.*64)
K/6th Penn. Cavalry – Cpt. Frederick Newhall (*c.*56)

1ST DIVISION

Brig.Gen. Wm. T. H. Brooks (*c.*8,073) Staff: *c.*6

1ST BRIGADE
Col. Alfred T. A. Torbert (*c.*2,576) Staff: 6
1st N. J. – Lt.Col. Mark W. Collet (*c.*358)
2nd N. J. – Col. Samuel L. Buck (*c.*406)
3rd N. J. – Col. Henry W. Brown (*c.*377)
4th N. J. – Col. William R. Hatch/Lt.Col. James Duffy (*c.*300)]
15th N. J. – Lt.Col. Edw. L. Campbell (*c.*573)
23rd N. J. – Lt.Col. Henry O. Ryerson (*c.*556)

Early in the war, in 1861, these United States Engineers were dressed like most troops of both sides, in regulation uniforms with dark cross belts, kepis, overcoats with capes, and a stripe up their pants leg. By 1862 the uniforms would have devolved into something more functional for field wear.

2ND BRIGADE
Col. Henry L. Cake (*c.*2,882) Staff: 2
27th N. Y. – Col. A. D. Adams (*c.*667)
121st N. Y. – Col. Emory Upton (*c.*691)
5th Maine – Col. E. A. Scammo (*c.*389)
16th N. Y. – Lt.Col. J. J. Seaver (*c.*745)
96th Penn. – Lt.Col. Peter A. Filbert (*c.*388)

3RD BRIGADE
Brig.Gen. David A. Russell (*c.*2,135) Staff: *c.*2
18th N. Y. – Col. George R. Myers (508)
31st N. Y. – Lt.Col. Leopold C. Newmann (*c.*502)
32nd N. Y. – Col. Francis E. Pinto/Cpt. Charles Hubbs (*c.*591)
95th Penn. – Lt.Col. Elisha Hall (*c.*532)

1ST DIVISION ARTILLERY (*c.*474)
D/2nd U.S. – 1st Lt. E. B. Williston (*c.*127) 6/12N
1st (A)/ N. J. Light Btty. (Hexamer's Btty.) – Cpt. Wm. Hexamer (*c.*99) 6/10P
A (1st)/Mass. Bttn. – Cpt. Wm. H. McCartney (*c.*137) 6/12N
A/Md. Light Arty. – Cpt. J. W. Wolcott (*c.*111) 6/3in.

2ND DIVISION

Brig.Gen. Albion P. Howe (*c.*7,741) Staff: 2

1ST BRIGADE
Brig.Gen. Calvin E. Pratt (*c.*2,555) Staff: *c.*2
5th Wisc. – Col. Amasa Cobb (*c.*613)
49th Penn. – Col. William F. Irwin (*c.*285)
6th Maine – Col. Hiram Burnham (*c.*547)
43rd N. Y. – Col. Benjamin F. Baker (*c.*576)
119th Penn. – Col. P. C. Ellmaker (*c.*532)

2ND BRIGADE
Col. Henry Whiting (*c.*2,874) Staff: 6
2nd Vermont – Col. Henry Whiting/Lt.Col. Chas. Joyce (*c.*584)
3rd Vermont – Col. Breed N. Hyde (540)
4th Vermont – Col. Chas.B. Stoughton (259)
5th Vermont – Col. Lewis A. Grant (448)
6th Vermont – Col. Nathan Lord Jr. (529)
26th N. J. – Col. A. J. Morrison (*c.*481)

3RD BRIGADE
Brig.Gen. Francis Vinton /Col. Robert Taylor/ Brig.Gen. Thomas Neill (*c.*1,892) Staff: *c.*16
33rd N. Y. – Col. Robert F. Taylor (*c.*281)
20th N. Y. – Col. Ernst van Vegesack (103)
49th N. Y. – Col. D. D. Bidwell (*c.*394)
77th N. Y. – Col. James B. McKean/Lt.Col. Windsor B. French (*c.*452)
21st N. J. – Col. Gilliam van Houten (*c.*323)

2ND DIVISION ARTILLERY (*c.*418)
F/5th US – Cpt. R. B. Ayres/1st Lt. Leonard Martin (*c.*125) 4/10H, 2/12H
B/Md. Light Arty. – Cpt. Alonzo Snow (*c.*102) 4/3R
1st N. Y. Light Btty. – Cpt. Andrew Cowan (*c.*103)6/3R
3rd N. Y. Light Btty. – Cpt. William Stewart/1st Lt. Wm. A. Harn (*c.*88) 4/10lb.

3RD DIVISION

Brig.Gen. John Newton (*c.*6,433) Staff: 3

1ST BRIGADE
Brig.Gen. John Cochrane (*c.*2,251) Staff: *c.*3
23rd Penn. – Col. T. H. Neill/Maj. John F. Glenn (*c.*528)

61st Penn. – Col. G. C. Spear (*c.*294)
82nd Penn. – Col. David H. Williams (*c.*326)
65th N. Y. (1st US Chasseurs) – Col. Alexander Shaler (*c.*319)
67th N. Y. (1st Long Island) – Lt.Col. Nelson Cross (*c.*378)
122nd N. Y. (3rd Onandaga) – Col. Silas Titus (*c.*403)

2ND BRIGADE
Brig.Gen. Charles Devens Jr. (*c.*2,322) Staff: 1
2nd R. I. – Col. Frank Wheaton (*c.*429)
36th N. Y. – Col. Wm. H. Browne (411)
7th Mass. – Col. Franklin P. Harlowe (*c.*470)
10th Mass. – Col. Henry L. Eustis (*c.*430)
37th Mass. – Col. Oliver Edwards (*c.*581)

3RD BRIGADE
Col. Thomas A. Rowley/Col. Frank Wheaton (*c.*1857) Staff: 1
62nd N. Y. (Anderson's Zouaves) – Maj. Wilson Hubbell (*c.*357)
93rd Penn. – Maj. John Mark (*c.*313)
98th Penn. – Lt.Col. Adolph Mehler (*c.*395)
102nd Penn. – Lt.Col. Joseph M. Kinkead (*c.*272)
139th Penn. – Lt.Col. James D. Owens (*c.*519)

3RD DIVISION ARTILLERY (*c.*231)
C/1st Penn. Light Btty. – Cpt. Jeremiah McCarthy (*c.*58) 4 /10lb.
D/1st Penn. Light Btty. – Cpt. Michael Hall (*c.*56) 4/10lb.
G/2nd US Arty – 1st Lt. John H. Butler (*c.*117) 6/12N

CAVALRY BRIGADE
Brig.Gen. George D. Bayard/Col. David McM. Gregg (*c.*517)
1st Penn. Cavalry – Col. Owen Jones (*c.*351)
10th N. Y. Cavalry – Lt.Col. William Irvine (501)
2nd N. Y. Cavalry – Maj. Henry E. Davies (*c.*264)
Independent Co., District of Columbia Cavalry – 1st Lt. Wm. Orton (*c.*58)
1st Maine Cavalry – Lt.Col. Calvin S. Douty (*c.*552)
1st N. J. – Lt.Col. Joseph Karge (*c.*199)

BTTY. C/3RD U.S. ARTY
Cpt. Horatio G. Gibson (*c.*144) 6/3R

CENTRE GRAND DIVISION

Maj.Gen. Joseph Hooker
Reported strength: 47,952 Staff: 6

III CORPS

Brig.Gen. George Stoneman (*c.*20,575) Staff: *c.*9

1ST DIVISION

Brig.Gen. David B. Birney (*c.*7,982) Staff: 4

1ST BRIGADE
Brig.Gen. John C. Robinson (*c.*2,475) Staff: *c.*2
20th Ind. – Col. John van Valkenburg (*c.*430)
63rd Penn. – Col. A. A. McKnight/Maj. John A. Danks (*c.*369)
68th Penn. – Col. Andrew H. Tippin (*c.*398)

105th Penn. – Col. Amor A. McKnight (*c.*361)
114th Penn. (Collis' Zouaves) – Col. C. H. T. Collis (*c.*468)
141st Penn. – Col. H. J. Madill (*c.*447)

2ND BRIGADE
Brig.Gen. J. H. Hobart Ward (*c.*2,498) Staff: 6
57th Penn. – Col. C. T. Campbell (*c.*351)
99th Penn. – Col. Asher S. Leidy (*c.*312)
3rd Maine – Col. Moses B. Lakeman (*c.*276)
4th Maine – Col. Elijah Walker (*c.*369)
55th N. Y. – Col. Regis P. de Trobriand (*c.*250)
38th N. Y. – Lt.Col. William Birney (*c.*374)
40th N. Y. (Mozart Reg't.) – Lt.Col. Thos. W. Egan {Lt.Col. N. A. Gesner } (*c.*560)

3RD BRIGADE
Brig.Gen. Hiram G. Berry (22,782) Staff: 1
5th Mich. – Lt.Col. John Gilluly/Maj. E. T. Sherlock (*c.*294)
37th N. Y. – Col. Samuel B. Hayman (*c.*734)
101st N. Y. – Col. Geo. F. Chester (*c.*300)
17th Maine – Col. Thos. A. Roberts (*c.*463)
1st N. Y. – Col. J. Frederick Pierson (*c.*680)
3rd Mich. – Lt.Col. Byron R. Pierce/Maj. Moses B. Houghton (*c.*310)

1ST DIVISION ARTILLERY
Cpt. George E. Randolph (*c.*223)
K&F/3rd U.S. Arty – Cpt. L. L. Livingston/1st Lt. John G. Turnbull (*c.*115) 6/12N
E/1st R. I. Light Arty – 1st Lt. P. S. Jastrom (*c.*108) 6/12N

2ND DIVISION

Brig.Gen. Daniel E. Sickles (*c.*7,192) Staff: 4

1ST BRIGADE
Brig.Gen. Joseph B. Carr (*c.*2,372) Staff: 2
11th Mass. – Col. W. Blaisdell (*c.*363)
16th Mass. – Col. Thos. R. Tannatt (*c.*323)
1st Mass. – Lt.Col. Clark B. Baldwin (*c.*419)
26th Penn. – Lt.Col. Benjamin C. Tilghman (*c.*463)
11th N. J. – Col. Robert McAllister (*c.*447)
2nd N. H. – Col. Gilman Marston (*c.*355)

2ND BRIGADE (EXCELSIOR BDE.)
Col. George B. Hall (*c.*2,156) Staff: 2
70th (1st Excelsior) N. Y. – Col. J. Egbert Farnum (*c.*321)
71st (2nd Excelsior) N. Y. – Maj. Thomas Rafferty (*c.*283)
72nd (3rd Excelsior) N. Y. – Col. William O. Stevens (*c.*408)
73rd (4th Excelsior) N. Y. – Col. William R. Brewster (*c.*387)
74th (5th Excelsior) N. Y. – Lt.Col. Wm. B. Lounsbury (*c.*306)
120th N. Y. – Col. George H. Sharpe (*c.*449)

3RD BRIGADE
Brig.Gen. Joseph W. Revere (*c.*2,123) Staff: 1
5th N. J. – Col. William J. Sewell (*c.*327)
6th N. J. – Col. Geo. C. Burling (*c.*274)
7th N. J. – Col. Louis R. Francine (*c.*323)
8th N. J. – Col. Adolphus J. Johnson (*c.*295)
2nd N. Y. – Col. Sydney W. Park (*c.*641)
115th Penn. – Lt.Col. Wm. A. Olmsted (*c.*262)

2ND DIVISION ARTILLERY
Cpt. James Smith (*c.*537)
K/4th US – 1st Lt. F. W. Seeley (*c.*179) 6/12N
H/1st US – 1st Lt. Justin E. Dimick (89) 6/12N
2nd N. J. Btty. – Cpt. A. J. Clark (*c.*153) 6/10P

4th Btty. (D), N. Y. Light Arty – Cpt. Joseph E. Nairn (c.116) 6/10P

3RD DIVISION
Brig.Gen. Amiel W. Whipple (c.3,592) Staff: 4

1ST BRIGADE
Brig.Gen. A. Sanders Piatt/Col. Emlen Franklin (c.1,448) Staff: 4
124th N. Y. – Col. A. V. Ellis (c.442)
86th N. Y. – Lt.Col. B. J. Chapman (c.365)
122nd Penn. – Col. Emlen Franklin (c.637)

2ND BRIGADE
Col. Samuel S. Carroll (c.1,750) Staff: c.2
84th Penn. – Col. Samuel M. Bowman (c.553)
110th Penn. – Lt.Col. J. Crowther (c.203)
163rd N. Y. – Maj. James J. Byrne (c.450)

*12th N. H. (*Independent Command) – Col. Joseph H. Potter (c.542)

3RD DIVISION ARTILLERY
(c.390)
11th Btty., N. Y. Light Arty – Cpt. A. A. von Puttkammer (c.149) 6/3R
10th N. Y. Light Btty. – Cpt. J. T. Bruen (c.116) 6/12N
H/1st Ohio – 1st Lt. Geo. W. Norton (c.125) 6/3R

V CORPS
Brig.Gen. Daniel Butterfield (c.28,500) Staff: 7

1ST DIVISION
Brig.Gen. Charles Griffin (c.17,603) Staff: 7

1ST BRIGADE
Col. James Barnes (c.2,227) Staff: 4
18th Mass. – Lt.Col. Joseph Hayes (c.329)
2nd Co. Mass. Sharpshooters – Cpt. Lewis E. Wentworth (c.37)
25th N. Y. – Cpt. Patrick Connelly (c.284)
13th N. Y. – Col. Elisha G. Marshall (c.556)
118th Penn. – Lt.Col. James Gwyn (c.460)
1st Mich. – Lt.Col. I. C. Abbott (c.175)
22nd Mass. (Henry Wilson's Reg't.) – Lt.Col. Wm. S. Tilton (2.152)
2nd Maine – Lt.Col. Geo. Varney (c.527)

2ND BRIGADE
Col. Jacob B. Sweitzer (c.2,134) Staff: 1
14th N. Y. – Lt.Col. Thos. W. Davies (c.618)
4th Mich. – Lt.Col. Geo. W. Lumbard (c.373)
9th Mass. – Col. Patrick R. Guiney (c.428)
32nd Mass. – Col. Francis J. Parker/Lt.Col. G.L. Prescott (c.258)
62nd Penn. – Lt.Col. J. C. Hull (c.456)

3RD BRIGADE
Col. T. B. W. Stockton (c.1,910) Staff: 1
1 12th N. Y. – Lt.Col. Robert M. Richardson (c.127)
17th N. Y. – Cpt. John Vickers (c.350)
44th N. Y. (People's Ellsworth Reg't.) – Lt.Col. F. Conner /Maj. Edw. B. Knox (c.407)
16th Mich. – Lt.Col. Norval E. Welch (c.283)
20th Maine – Col. Adelbert Ames (c.390)
83rd Penn. – Col. Strong Vincent (c.299)
Mich. Sharpshooters (Brady's Co.) – 1st Lt. Jonas H. Titus Jr. (c.53)

1ST DIVISION ARTILLERY
Cpt. A. P. Martin (c.429)

3rd (C) /Mass. Light Btty. – 1st Lt. V. M. Drum (c.124) 6/12N
5th (E)/ Mass. Light Btty. – Cpt. Charles A. Phillips (c.104) 6/3R
C/1st R. I. – Cpt. Richard Waterman (c.133) 6/3R
D/5th US Arty – 1st Lt. Chas. E. Hazlett (c.68) 6/10lb.

2ND DIVISION
Brig.Gen. George Sykes (c.5,001) Staff: 3

1ST BRIGADE
Lt.Col. Robert C. Buchanan (c.1,335) Staff: 2
3rd US – Cpt. John D. Wilkins (c.309)
4th US – Cpt. Hiram Dryer (c.177)
1st Bttn., 12th US – Cpt. Matthew M. Blunt (c.218)
2nd Bttn., 12th US – Cpt. Thos. M. Anderson (c.220)
1st Bttn., 14th US – Cpt. John D. O'Connell (256)
2nd Bttn., 14th US – Cpt. Giles B. Overton (153)

2ND BRIGADE
Maj. George L. Andrews/Maj. Charles Lovell (c.1,290) Staff: 2
11th US – Cpt. Chas. S. Russell (c.314)
Bttn. Of 1st & 2nd US – Cpt. Salem S. Marsh (299)
Bttn. Of 6th US – Cpt. Levi C. Bootes (c.178)
Bttn. Of 7th US – Cpt. David P. Hancock (c.132)
Bttn. Of 10th US – Cpt. Henry E. Maynadier (c.105)
Bttn. of 17th & 19th US – Cpt. John P. Wales (c.260)
1st US Sharpshooters – Lt.Col. Casper Trepp (c.313)

3RD BRIGADE
Brig.Gen. Gouverneur K. Warren (c.1,860) Staff: 2
5th N. Y. – Col. Cleveland Winslow (c.735)
140th N. Y. – Col. Patrick H. O'Rorke (c.547)
146th N. Y. – Col. Kenner Garrard (c.584)
2nd Division Arty – 1st Lt. M.F. Watson (c.200)
I/5th US Arty – Cpt. Weed/1st Lt. Malbone F. Watson (c.76) 4/3R
L/1st Ohio – 1st Lt. Frederick Dorries (c.124) 6/12N

3RD DIVISION
Brig.Gen. Andrew A. Humphreys (c.4,667) Staff: 5

1ST BRIGADE
Brig.Gen. Erastus B. Tyler (2,201) Staff: c.2
91st Penn. – Col. Edgar M. Gregory (424)
134th Penn. – Lt.Col. Edward O'Brien (542)
126th Penn. – Col. James G. Elder/Lt.Col. David W. Rowe (632)
129th Penn. – Col. Jacob G. Frick (601)

2ND BRIGADE
Col. Peter H. Allabach (c.2,139) Staff: 2
131st Penn. – Lt.Col. Wm. B. Shunt (c.510)
123rd Penn. – Col. John B. Clark (c.675)
133rd Penn. – Col. Franklin B. Speakman (c.576)
155th Penn. – Col. Edw. J. Allen (c.376)
3rd Division Artillery – Cpt. Alanson M. Randol (c.322)
E&G/1st US Artillery – Cpt. Alanson M. Randol (234) 4/12lb.

Section C/1st N. Y. Light Arty – 1st Lt. Wm. H. Phillips (c.88) 6/3R

CAVALRY BRIGADE
Brig.Gen. William Averell (c.1,228) Staff: 2
1st Mass. – Col. Horace B. Sargent (78)
3rd Penn. – Lt.Col. Edw. S. Jones (156)
4th Penn. – Col. James K. Kerr (104)
5th US Cavalry – Cpt. James E. Harrison (c.345)
B&L/ 2nd US Arty – Cpt. James M. Robertson (c.99)4/3R

RIGHT GRAND DIVISION
Maj.Gen. E. V. Sumner
Reported strength: 37,432

II CORPS
Maj.Gen. Darius N. Couch (c.15,664) Staff: 6

1ST DIVISION
Brig.Gen. Winfield Scott Hancock (c.5,006) Staff: NA

1ST BRIGADE
Brig.Gen. John C. Caldwell/Col. George von Schack (1,994) Staff: c.2
61st N. Y. (Clinton Guards) – Col. Nelson A. Miles combined with
64th N. Y. (1st Catteraugus Reg't.) – Col. Enos C. Brooks/ Cpt. Harvey L. Jones (435 total)
145th Penn. – Col. Hiram L. Brown (505)
5th N. H. – Col. Edw. E. Cross (303)
81st Penn. – Lt.Col. H. Boyd McKeen/Cpt. Wm. Wilson (261)
7th N. Y. – Col. George von Shack/Cpt. G. A. Von Bransen (488)

2ND BRIGADE (IRISH BRIGADE)
Brig.Gen. Thomas F. Meagher (1317) Staff: c.2
69th N. Y. – Col. Robert Nugent/Cpt. James Saunders (238)
88th N. Y. – Col. Patrick Kelly (252)
63rd N. Y. – Lt.Col. Richard C. Bentley/ Maj. Joseph O'Neill (162)
28th Mass. – Col. Richard Byrnes (416)
116th Penn. – Col. Dennis Heenan/Lt.Col. St. Clair A. Mulholland (247)

3RD BRIGADE
Col. Samuel K. Zook (c.1,534) Staff: c.2
57th N. Y. (National Guard Rifles) – Lt.Col. Alford B. Chapman/ Maj. N. G. Throop (192)
53rd Penn. – Col. John R. Brooke (314)
2nd Del. – Col. Wm. P. Bailey (244)
52nd N. Y. (German Rangers) – Col. Paul Frank (160)
66th N. Y. (Governor's Guard) – Lt.Col. James H. Bull/Cpt. Julius Wehle (238)
27th Conn. – Col. Richard S. Bostwick (384)

1ST DIVISION ARTILLERY
(c.300)
C/4th US – 1st Lt. Evan Thomas (217) 6/12lb.
B/1st N. Y. Light Arty – Cpt. Rufus D. Pettit (173) 6/10lb.

2ND DIVISION

Brig.Gen. Oliver O. Howard (c.5,566) Staff: 11

1ST BRIGADE

Brig.Gen. Alfred Sully (c.1,975) Staff: 2
34th N. Y. – Col. James A. Suiter (c.270)
1st Company Mass. Sharpshooters – Cpt. Wm. Plumer (c.51)
15th Mass. – Maj. Chase Philbrick (498)
82nd (2nd Militia) N. Y. – Col. James Huston (c.298)
19th Maine – Col. Frederick D. Sewell (c.446)
1st Minn. – Col. Geo. N. Morgan (c.344)
2nd Company Minn. Sharpshooters – Cpt. Wm. F. Russell (c.66)

2ND BRIGADE

Col. Joshua T. Owen (c.1,362) Staff: c.2
69th Penn. – Lt.Col. Denis O'Kane (c.323)
71st Penn. – Lt.Col. John Markoe (c.302)
72nd Penn. – Col. DeWitt C. Baxter (c.416)
106th Penn. – Col. Turner G. Morehead (c.319)

3RD BRIGADE

Col. Norman J. Hall (c.1,958) Staff: c.2
20th Mass. – Cpt. George N. Macy (238)
19th Mass. – Cpt. H. G. Weymouth {J. F. Plimpton} (355)
42nd N. Y. – Lt.Col. Geo. N. Bomford (c.287)
127th Penn. – Col. Wm. W. Jennings (c.565)
7th Mich. – Lt.Col. Henry Baxter (c.147)
59th N. Y. – Lt.Col. William Northedge (c.363)

2ND DIVISION ARTILLERY

(c.260)
A/1st R. I. Light Arty– Cpt. William A. Arnold (c.119) 6/3R
B/1st R. I. Arty – Cpt. Jophn G. Hazard/1st Lt. Evan Thomas (c.141) 6/12lb.

3RD DIVISION

Brig.Gen. William H. French (c.4,847) Staff: 3

1ST BRIGADE

Brig.Gen. Nathan Kimball/Col. John S. Mason (c.2,124) Staff: c.4
4th Ohio – Col. John S. Mason/Lt.Col. James H. Godman (113)
14th Ind. – Maj. Elijah H. C. Cavins (c.290)
7th Va. (W.Va.) – Col. Joseph Snider (c.275)
8th Ohio – Lt.Col. Franklin Sawyer (c.298)
24th N. J. – Col. Wm. B. Robertson (c.479)
28th N. J. – Col. M. N. Wisewell (665)

2ND BRIGADE

Col. Oliver H. Palmer (c.974) Staff: c.2
14th Conn. – Lt.Col. Sanford H. Perkins (c.261)
108th N. Y. (Rochester Reg't.) – Lt.Col. Chas. J. Powers (c.295)
130th Penn. – Col. H. I. Zinn (c.416)

3RD BRIGADE

Lt.Col. John W. Andrews/Lt.Col. Wm. Jameson (c.1,486) Staff: c.1
132nd Penn. – Lt.Col. Charles Albright (251)
4th N. Y. – Col. John D. McGregor (c.476)
1st Del. – (Col. J.W. Andrews)/Maj. Thomas A. Smyth (c.544)
10th N. Y. (National Zouaves) – Col. John E. Bendix (214)

3RD DIVISION ARTILLERY

(c.260)
G/1st N. Y. Arty – Cpt. John D. Frank (c.110)6/12lb.
G/1st R. I. – Cpt. Chas. D. Owen (c.150) 6/3R
II Corps Reserve Artillery – Cpt. Charles Morgan (c.239) Staff: NA
I/1st US Arty – 1st Lt. Edmund Kirby (c.113) 6/12lb.
A/4th US Arty – 1st Lt. Rufus King (c.126) 6/3R

IX CORPS

Brig.Gen. Orlando B. Wilcox (c.16,614) Staff: c.8

ESCORT

B/6th N. Y. Cavalry – Cpt. Hillman A. Hall (c.33)
C/6th N. Y. Cavalry – Cpt. William A. Heernance (c.32)

1ST DIVISION

Brig.Gen. Wm. W. Burns (c.6,950) Staff: 4

1ST BRIGADE

Col. Orlando M. Poe (NA) Staff: 3
79th N. Y. – Lt.Col. David Morrison (NA)
2nd Mich. – Lt.Col. Louis Dillman (NA)
17th Mich. – Col. Wm. H. Withington (NA)
20th Mich. – Col. Adolphus W. Williams (NA)

2ND BRIGADE

Col. Benjamin C. Christ (NA) Staff: NA
29th Mass. – Lt.Col. Joseph H. Barnes (NA)
8th Mich. – Maj. Ralph Ely (NA)
27th N. J. – Col. Geo. W. Mindil (NA)
46th N. Y. – Lt.Col. Joseph Gerhardt (c.262)
50th Penn. – Lt.Col. Thos. Brenholtz (NA)

3RD BRIGADE

Col. Daniel Leasure (NA) Staff: NA
45th Penn. – Col. Thomas Welsh (NA)
100th Penn. – Lt.Col. David A. Leckey (NA)
36th Mass. – Col. Henry Bowman (NA)

1ST DIVISION ARTILLERY

Cpt. John Edwards (c.227)
D/1st N. Y. – Cpt. Thos. W. Osborn (c.109) 6/12lb.
L&M/3rd US Arty – Cpt. Edwards/1st Lt. Horace J. Hayden (c.118) 4/10lb., 2/12lb.

2ND DIVISION

Brig.Gen. Samuel D. Sturgis (c.4,849) Staff: NA

1ST BRIGADE

Brig.Gen. James Nagle (NA) Staff: NA
6th N. H. – Col. Simon Griffin (264)
7th R. I. – Col. Zenas R. Bliss (NA)
2nd Md. – Col. Thos. B. Allard/Maj. H. Howard (NA)
48th Penn. – Col. Joshua K. Sigfried (NA)
12th R. I. – Col. George H. Browne (NA)
9th N. H. – Col. E. R. Fellows/Lt.Col. John Babbitt (NA)

2ND BRIGADE

Brig.Gen. Edward Ferrero (1,930) Staff: NA
51st Penn. – Col. John F. Hartranft (NA)
21st Mass. – Lt.Col. Wm. S. Clark (284)
51st N. Y. – Col. Robert B. Potter (NA)
35th Mass. – Lt.Col. S. Carruth/Maj. Sidney Willard (NA)
11th N. H. – Col. Walter Harriman (NA)

2ND DIVISION ARTILLERY

(c.430)
E/4th US Arty – 1st Lt. George Dickenson (c.62) 4/10P
D/1st R. I. – Cpt. Wm. W. Buckley (c.121) 4/12lb.
L/2nd N. Y. Light Arty – Cpt. Jacob Roemer (c.125) 4/3R
2nd (D)Penn. Light – Cpt. Geo. W. Durrell (c.122) 6/10lb.

3RD DIVISION

Brig.Gen. George W. Getty (c.4,204) Staff: 2

1ST BRIGADE

Col. Rush C. Hawkins (c.2,015) Staff: 2
9th N. Y. – Maj. E. A. Kimball (c.367)
89th N. Y. – Col. Harrison S. Fairchild (NA)
103rd N. Y. – Maj. Benjamin Ringold (NA)
10th N. H. – Col. Michael T. Donohoe (NA)
13th N. H. – Col. Aaron F. Stevens (NA)
25th N. J. – Col. Andrew Derrom (NA)

2ND BRIGADE

Col. Edward Harland (c.1,963) Staff: c.2
4th R. I. – Maj. Martin P. Buffom (NA)
21st Conn. – Col. Arthur H. Dutton (NA)
8th Conn. – Maj. John E. Ward (NA)
11th Conn. – Col. Griffin A. Stedman Jr. (500)
15th Conn. – Lt.Col. Samuel Tolles (NA)
16th Conn. – Col. Frank Beach/ Capt. C. Upham (NA)

3RD DIVISION ARTILLERY

(c.226)
E/2nd US – 1st Lt. Samuel N. Benjamin (c.127) 6/20lb.
A/5th US – 1st Lt. J. Gillis (c.99) 6/12lb.

CAVALRY DIVISION

Brig.Gen. Alfred Pleasonton (c.2,802) Staff: 11

1ST BRIGADE

Brig.Gen. John F. Farnsworth (c.1,398) Staff: 4
8th N. Y. – Col. Benjamin F. Davis (c.585)
3rd Ind. (45th Ind. Volunteers) – Maj. Geo. H. Chapman (c.337)
8th Ill. – Col. Wm. Gamble (c.472)

2ND BRIGADE

Col. David McM. Gregg /Col. Thos. C. Devin (c.1,276) Staff: 5
8th Penn. – Lt.Col. Amos E. Griffiths (c.496)
6th US – Cpt. Geo. C. Cram (c.482)
6th N. Y. – Col. Thomas C. Devin/Lt.Col. Duncan McVicar (c.293)

ARTILLERY

M/2nd US – Cpt. A. C. M. Pennington Jr. (c.117) 6/3R

AT AQUIA CREEK/ BELLE PLAIN

21st N. J.
22nd N. J.
29th N. J.
30th N. J.
31st N. J.
147th N. Y.
137th Penn.

ARMY OF NORTHERN VIRGINIA

Gen. Robert E. Lee
(Reported strength: 85,175) Staff: 17
Chief of Staff: Col. Robert H. Chilton
Chief Engineer: Col. W. P. Smith
Provost Marshal: Maj. Cornelius Boyle/Maj. Daniel
    Bridgeford
1st Va. Regular Bttn. –
Upshaw's Va. Cavalry Co. – Cpt. Thomas E.
    Upshaw (NA)

I CORPS (LONGSTREET'S CORPS)

Lt. Gen. James Longstreet (Reported strength:
38,320) Staff: 13
Provost Marshal: Lt.Col. R. P. Blount

McLAWS' DIVISION

Maj.Gen. Lafayette McLaws (Reported strength:
9,285) Staff: 35

BARKSDALE'S BRIGADE
Brig.Gen. William Barksdale (1,598) Staff: 4
13th Miss. – Col. James W. Carter (204)
17th Miss. – Lt.Col. John C. Fiser (277)
18th Miss. – Col. Wm. H. Leese (192)
21st Miss. – Col. Benjamin G. Humphreys (270

KERSHAW'S BRIGADE
Brig.Gen. Joseph B. Kershaw (2,077) Staff: 6
2nd (Palmetto) S. C. – Col. John D. Kennedy
    (350)
3rd S. C. – Col. James D. Nance (400)
3rd S. C. Volunteers – Lt.Col. Wm. Rice (282)
7th S. C. – Col. Elbert Bland (353)
8th S. C. – Col. E. T. Stackhouse (282)
15th S. C. – Col. Wm. De Saussure (404)

SEMMES' BRIGADE
Brig.Gen. Paul J. Semmes (1,464) Staff: 4
10th Ga. – Col. John B. Weems (151)
53rd Ga. – Col. James P. Simms (265)
50th Ga. – Col. Wm. P. Manning (528)
51st Ga. – Col. Edward Ball/ Col. Robert
    McMillan (516)

COBB'S (IRISH) BRIGADE
Brig.Gen. Thomas R. R. Cobb/Col. Robert
McMillan (1,486) Staff: 4
Cobb's Ga. Legion – Lt.Col. Luther Glenn (392)
16th Ga. – Col. Goode Bryan (181)
24th Ga. – Col. Robert McMillan (166)
18th Ga. – Col. William T. Wofford/Lt.Col. Solon
    Z. Ruff (415)
Phillips Ga. Legion – Col. B. F. Cook (328)

DIVISION ARTILLERY
Col. Henry C. Cabell (c.416)
A/1st N. C. (Ellis' Flying Artillery) Artillery
    Btty. – Cpt. Basil C. Manly (c.143) 2/12H;
    3/6SB; 1/3R
Read's Pulaski Ga. Btty. – Cpt. John P. W.
    Read (78) 1/10P; 1/12H; 1/3R
1st Company Richmond Howitzers – Cpt.
    Edward S. McCarthy (c.94) 2/10P; 2/6SB
Troup Ga. Artillery – Cpt. Henry H. Carlton
    (c.101) 2/10P; 2/3R

ANDERSON'S DIVISION

Maj.Gen. Richard Anderson/ Maj.Gen. Cadmus
Wilcox (Reported strength: 9,373) Staff: 23

WILCOX'S BRIGADE
Maj.Gen. Cadmus Wilcox (2,253) Staff: 5
8th Ala. – Col. Young L. Royster (c.523)
9th Ala. – Col. Samuel Henry (c.418)
10th Ala. – Col. William H. Forney (c.411)
11th Ala. – Col. John C. C. Saunders (c.429)
14th Ala. – Lt.Col. Lucius Pinckard (467)

PERRY'S BRIGADE
Brig.Gen. Edward Perry (c.813) Staff: 3
2nd Fla. – Col. L. G. Pyles (c.277)
5th Fla. – Col. John G. Hatley (c.342)
8th Fla. – Col. David Lang (c.191)

FEATHERSTON'S BRIGADE
Brig.Gen. Winfield S. Featherston (1,628) Staff: 4
12th Miss. – Col. William H. Taylor (c.374)
16th Miss. – Col. Carnot Posey (c.496)
19th Miss. – Col. Nathan H. Harris (c.425)
5 companies/48th Miss. – Col. Joseph M.
    Jayne (c.329)

WRIGHT'S BRIGADE
Brig.Gen. Ambrose R. Wright (c.1,628) Staff: 4
3rd Ga. – Col. Edward J. Walker (c.581)
22nd Ga. – Col. Robert H. Jones (c.450)
48th Ga. – Col. William Gibson (467)
2nd Ga. Bttn. – Cpt. Charles J. Muffett (200)

MAHONE'S BRIGADE
Brig.Gen. Wm. Mahone/Col. Parham (c.1,851)
Staff: 4
6th Va. – Col. George T. Rogers (335)
12th Va. – Col. David A. Weisiger (c.434)
16th Va. – Col. Joseph H. Ham (489)
41st Va. – Col. William A. Parham (328)
61st Va. – Col. Virginmius D. Groner (261)

ANDERSON'S DIVISION ARTILLERY – (c.429)
Donaldsville La. Arty. – Cpt. Victor Maurin
    (c.115) 2/10P; 1/3R; 3/6SB
Huger's (Norfolk)Va. Btty. – Cpt. Frank Huger
    (106) 1/3R; 1/10P; 2/6SB
Pittsylvania Btty. – Cpt. John Lewis (97) 2/3R;
    2/10P
Norfolk Light Artillery Blues – Cpt. Charles R.
    Grandy (c.111) 2/12H; 2/3R; 2/10P; 2/6SB

PICKETT'S DIVISION

Maj.Gen. George Pickett
(Reported strength: 9,001) Staff: 22

ARMISTEAD'S BRIGADE
Brig.Gen. Lewis Armistead (c.2,046) Staff: 4
9th Va. – Col. J. C. Owens (c.257)
14th Va. – Col. James G. Hodges (c.424)
38th Va. – Col. Edward C. Edmunds (c.356)
53rd Va. – Col. Harrison B. Tomlin (c.435)
57th Va. – Col. George W. Carr (c.470)

CORSE'S BRIGADE
Brig.Gen. Montgomery D. Corse (NA) Staff: c.3
15th Va. – Col. Emmett M. Morrison (115)
17th Va. – Col. Morton Marye/Lt.Col. Arthur
    Herbert ( )
30th Va. – Col. A. T. Harrison ( )
32nd Va. – Col. E. B. Montague (143)

KEMPER'S BRIGADE
Brig.Gen. James L. Kemper (c.1,445) Staff: 11
1st Va. Col. Lewis B. Williams (c.211)
3rd Va. – Col. Joseph Mayo Jr. (c.332)
7th Va. – Col. Waller T. Patton (c.337)
11th Va. – Col. Kirkwood Otey (c.357)
24th Va. – Col. William R. Terry (c.497)

GARNETT'S BRIGADE
Brig.Gen. Richard B. Garnett (c.1,477) Staff: 4
8th Va. – Col. Eppa Hunton (c.204)
18th Va. – Lt.Col. George C. Cabell (c.314)
19th Va. – Col. Henry Gantt (c.330)
28th Va. – Col. Robert C. Allen (c.335)
56th Va. – Col. William D. Stuart (c.290)

JENKINS' BRIGADE
Brig.Gen. Micah Jenkins/ Col. Walker (NA) Staff:
4
1st S. C. – Col. William H. Duncan (c.432)
2nd S. C. Rifles – Col. Thomas Thomason
    (c.413)
5th S. C. – Col. Ashbury Coward (NA)
6th S. C. – Col. John Bratton (NA)
Palmetto Sharpshooters – Col. Joseph Walker
    (NA)
Hampton's Legion – Col. Martin W. Gary (NA)

PICKETT'S DIVISION ARTILLERY
Cpt. James Dearing (c.322)
Fauquier Btty. – Cpt. Robert M. Stribling
    (c.135) 2/24H; 4/12N
D/38th (Dearing's) Virgina Btty. – Cpt. Joseph
    G. Blount (c.96) 1/10P; 1/12H; 2/6SB
I/1st Va. (Richmond) Artillery – Cpt. Miles C.
    Macon (c.91) 2/10P; 1/12H; 4/6SB

RANSOM'S DIVISION

Brig.Gen. Robert Ransom Jr. (Reported strength:
4,394) Staff: 5

RANSOM'S BRIGADE
Brig.Gen. Robert Ransom Jr. (NA) Staff: 3
24th N. C. – Col. William I. Clarke (NA)
25th N. C. – Col. Henry M. Rutledge (NA)
35th N. C. – Col. Matthew W. Ransom (NA)
49th N. C. – Col. Leroy M. McAfee (NA)
Branch's Va. Btty. – Cpt. James R. Branch
    (NA)

COOKE'S BRIGADE
Brig.Gen. Edwin D. Cooke/Col. Edward D. Hall
(NA) Staff:
15th N. C. – Col. Henry A. Dowd (NA)
27th N. C. – Col. John Gilmer Jr. (NA)
46th N. C. – Col. Edward D. Hall (NA)
48th N. C. – Lt.Col. Samuel H. Walkup (NA)
Cooper's Va. Btty. – Cpt. Thomas B. French
    (NA) 3/10P

HOOD'S DIVISION

Maj.Gen. John Bell Hood (Reported strength: 8,569)
Staff: 16

TOOMB'S BRIGADE
Gen. Toombs/Col. H. L. Benning (c.1,414) Staff: 4
2nd Ga. – Col. Edgar M. Butt (c.348)
15th Ga. – Col. Dudley McIvar DuBose (c.370)
17th Ga. – Col. Henry L. Benning (c.351)
20th Ga. – Col. John B. Cumming (c.341)

G.T. ANDERSON'S BRIGADE
General Evans (NA) Staff: 10
1st Ga. Regulars – Col. William J. Magill (NA)

7th Ga. – Col. Wm. W. White (*c*.378)
8th Ga. – Col. Lucius M. Lamar (*c*.313)
9th Ga. – Col. Benjamin Beck (*c*.341)
11th Ga. – Col. Francis H. Little (*c*.310)

LAWS' BRIGADE
Brig.Gen. Evander M. Law (NA) Staff: 4
4th Ala. – Col. Pickney D. Bowles (*c*.353)
6th N. C. – Col. Samuel McD. Tate (*c*.519)
44th Ala. – Col. Chas. A. Derby (*c*.363)
54th N. C. – Col. J. C. S. McDowell (NA)
57th N. C. – Col. A. C. Goodwin (*c*.374)

ROBERTSON'S BRIGADE
Brig.Gen. James B. Robertson (*c*.1,736) Staff: 5
3rd Ark. – Col. Samuel G. Earl (*c*.479)
1st Texas – Col. A. T. Ramsey (*c*.427)
4th Texas – Col. J. C. G. Key (*c*.416)
5th Texas – Col. R. M. Powell (*c*.409)

HOOD'S DIVISION ARTILLERY – (*c*.282)
German S. C. Artillery – Cpt. Wm. K. Bachman (*c*.71) 4/12N
Palmetto S. C. Light Artillery – Cpt. Hugh R. Garden (*c*.63) 1/12H; 1/12N; 2/6SB
Rowan N. C. Arty. – Cpt. James Reilly (*c*.148) 2/10P; 2/3R; 2/24H

I CORPS ARTILLERY – (*c*.901)

WALTON'S ARTILLEY BTTN. OF WASHINGTON LA. ARTILLERY
Col. J. B. Walton (*c*.329)
1st Co. Washington La. Arty. – Cpt. C. W. Squires (*c*.77) 2/3R; 1/10P
2nd Co./Washington La. Arty. – Cpt. J. B. Richardson (80) 2/12H; 2/12N
3rd Co./Washington La. Arty. – Cpt. M. B. Miller (*c*.92) 2/12N
4th Co./Washington La. Arty. – Cpt. B. F. Eschelman (*c*.81) 2/12H; 2/12N

ALEXANDER'S BATTALION
Lt.Col. E. Porter Alexander (415)
Bedford's Va. Btty. – Cpt. Tyler C. Jordan (*c*.78) 2/3R; 1/12H; 1/6SB
Rhett's S. C. Btty. – Cpt. A. B. Rhett (*c*.71) 2/20P; 2/10P
Eubank's Va. Btty. – Cpt. J. L. Eubank (95) 1/3R; 1/12H; 1/6SB
Parker's Va. Btty. – Cpt. William W. Parker (*c*.90) 2/3R; 2/12H
Ashland Artillery Btty. – Cpt. Pichegru Woolfolk Jr. (103) 2/20P; 2/12N
Madison (La.) Light Arty. – Cpt. Geo. V. Moody (135) 2/3R; 2/24H

II CORPS

Lt.Gen. Thomas J. (Stonewall) Jackson (NA) Staff: 13

JACKSON'S DIVISION

Brig.Gen. William B. Taliaferro (Reported: 6,067) Staff: 14

1ST (OR STONEWALL) BRIGADE
Brig.Gen. E. F. Paxton (1,619) Staff: 4
2nd Va. – Col. J. Q. Adams Nadenbousch (406)
4th Va. – Col. Charles A. Ronald (429)
5th Va. – Col. John H. S. Funk (263)
27th Va. – Col. James K. Edmondson (221)
33rd Va. – Col. Edwin G. Lee (296)

2ND (OR J.R. JONES') BRIGADE
Brig.Gen. John R. Jones (*c*.6,015) Staff: 7
21st Va. – Col. William A. Witcher (226)
42nd Va. – Col. Robert W. Withers (407)
48th Va. – Col. Thomas S. Garnett (377)
1st Va. Bttn.Provisionals (Irish) – Maj. David B. Bridgeford (*c*.123)

3RD (OR TALIAFERRO'S) BRIGADE
Col. E. T. H. Warren (*c*.1,993) Staff: 5
23rd Va. – Col. Alexander G. Taliferro (334)
47th Ala. – Cpt. J. M. Campbell (348)
48th Ala. – Cpt. C. B. St. John (374)
37th Va. – Cpt. Titus Vespasian Williams (*c*.399)
10th Va. – Cpt. W. B. Yancy (*c*.533)

4TH (OR PENDLETON'S) BRIGADE
Col. Edmund Pendleton (NA) Staff: 3
1st La. Volunteers – Lt.Col. James Nolan (*c*.220)
2nd La. – Maj. M. A. Grogan (*c*.364)
10th La. – Maj. John M. Leggett (*c*.313)
15th La. – Lt.Col. McG. Goodwyn (290)
14th La. – Cpt. H. M. Verlander (362)
Coppen's 1st La. Zouave Bttn. – Lt.Col. Geo. A. C. Coppens (NA)

ARTILLERY
Cpt. J. B. Brockenbrough (370)
Carpenter's Va. Btty. – 1st Lt. Geo. McKendree (95) 2/3R; 21/12N
Danville Va. Btty. – Cpt. G. W. Wooding (*c*.114) 2 /10P; 1/3R; 1/12N
Hampden Va. Btty. – Cpt. Wm. H. Caskie (*c*.90) 1/10P; 1/3R; 1/12N
Lee Va. Arty. – Cpt. Charles I. Raine (*c*.94) 3/3R; 1/12H
2nd Rockbridge Lusk Va. Arty. – Cpt. John A. M. Lusk (*c*.72) 1/10P; 1/3R; 2/6SB

EWELL'S DIVISION

Brig.Gen. Jubal A. Early (Reported strength: 9,209) Staff: 29

LAWTON'S BRIGADE
Col. Edmund N. Atkinson/Col. Clement Evans (*c*.2,205) Staff: 6
13th Ga. – Col. James M. Smith (395)
26th Ga. – Cpt. B. F. Grace (356)
31st Ga. – Col. Clement A. Evans (*c*.309)
38th Ga. – Cpt. Wm. L. McLeod (396)
60th Ga. – Col. William H. Stiles (*c*.372)
61st Ga. – Col. John H. Lamar (*c*.371)

EARLY'S BRIGADE
Col. James A. Walker (NA) Staff: *c*.4
13th Va. – Lt.Col. J. B. Terrill (332)
25th Va. – Col. Geo. H. Smith/ Lt.Col. John C. Higginbotham (NA)
31st Va. – Col. John S. Hoffman (NA)
44th Va. – Col. William C. Scott (NA)
49th Va. – Col. William SmithCol. J. C. Gibson (*c*.316)
52nd Va. – Col. Michael G. Harmon (*c*.271)
58th Va. – Col. Francis M. Board (641)

HAYS' (1ST LA. IRISH) BRIGADE
Brig.Gen. Harry T. Hays (NA) Staff: 3
5th La. – Col. Henry Forno (*c*.274)
6th La. – Col. William Monoghan (*c*.402)
7th La. – Col. Davidson B. Penn (*c*.355)
8th La. – Col. Henry B. Kelly (*c*.467)
9th La. – Col. Leroy A. Stafford (*c*.469)

TRIMBLE'S BRIGADE
Col. R.F. Hoke (NA)
12th Ga. – Col. Edward Willis (NA)
21st Ga. – Lt.Col. Thomas W. Hooper (NA)
15th Ala. – Col. James Cantey (NA)
1st N. C. Bttn. – Maj. Rufus W. Wharton (114)
21st N. C. – Col. William W. Kirkland (*c*.571)

EWELL'S DIVISIONAL ARTILLERY
Cpt. James W. Latimer (486)
Charlottesville Va. Btty. – Cpt. J. M. Carrington (*c*.77) 2/3R; 2/12H; 2/6SB
Chesapeake Md. Btty. – 1st Lt. John E. Plater (*c*.81) 2/10P; 1/3R
1st Md. Btty. – Cpt. Wm. F. Dement (*c*.99) 4/6SB
La. Guard Artillery – Cpt. Louis E. D'Aquin (68) 1/10P; 2/3R
Staunton Va. Btty. – 1st Lt. Asher W. Garber (*c*.65) 4/6SB
Courtney Va. Btty. – Cpt. Joseph W. Latimer (*c*.96) 2/3R; 2/12N

THE LIGHT (A. P. HILL'S) DIVISION

Maj.Gen. Ambrose P. Hill (Reported strength: 11,533) Staff: 30

4TH (OR LANE'S) BRIGADE
Brig.Gen. J. H. Lane (2,782) Staff: 4
7th N. C. – Col. Edward G. Haywood (*c*.526)
18th N. C. – Col. J. T. Purdie (*c*.532)
28th (Bethel Reg't.) N. C. – Col. Samuel D. Lowe (*c*.481)
33rd N. C. – Col. Clark M. Avery (*c*.586)
37th N. C. – Col. William M. Barbour (*c*.653)

2ND (OR GREGG'S) BRIGADE
Brig.Gen. Maxcy Gregg /Col. D. H. Hamilton (*c*.1,986) Staff: 4
1st S. C. (Orr's) Rifles – Col. James M. Perrin (194)
1st Provisional S. C. – Col. Daniel H. Hamilton Sr. (*c*.461)
12th S. C. – Col. Cadwallader Jones (*c*.37)
13th S. C. – Col. Oliver E. Edwards (*c*.498)
14th S. C. – Col. Samuel McGowan (*c*.459)

1ST (OR FIELD'S) BRIGADE
Col. J.M. Brockenborough (*c*.1,310) Staff: 4
22nd Va. Bttn.Reserves – Lt.Col. E. P. Tayloe (290)
40th Va. – Lt.Col.V. A. S. Cunningham (347)
55th Va. – Col. Francis Mallory (*c*.391)
47th Va. – Col. Robert M. Mayo (*c*.278)

6TH (OR PENDER'S) BRIGADE
Brig.Gen. William D. Pender/Col. Alfred Scales (*c*.1,879) Staff: 4
13th N. C. – Col. Alfred Scales (*c*.462)
16th N. C. – Col. John Smith McElroy/Col. William A. Stowe (*c*.444)
22nd N. C. – Maj. Christopher C. Cole (*c*.453)
34th N. C. – Col. Wm. L. J. Lowrance (154)
38th N. C. – Col. William J. Hoke (*c*.332)

5TH (OR ARCHER'S) BRIGADE
Brig.Gen. James J. Archer/Col. Peter Turney (*c*.1,621) Staff: 4
1st Tennessee – Lt.Col. Newton J. George (*c*.347)
7th Tennessee – Col. John F. Goodner (401)
14th Tennessee – Col. William McComb/Lt.Col. J. W. Lockert (*c*.274)
19th Ga. – Col. Andrew J. Hutchins (391)

5th Ala. Bttn. – Maj. Albert S. van de Graaf (204)

3RD (OR THOMAS') BRIGADE
Brig.Gen. Edward L. Thomas (c.1,633) Staff: 4
14th Ga. – Col. Robert W. Folsom (455)
35th Ga. – Col. Bolling H. Holt (397)
45th Ga. – Col. Thomas J. Simmons (c.388)
49th Ga. – Col. Andrew Jackson Lane (389)

A. P. HILL'S DIVISION ARTILLERY
Maj. R. L. Walker (607)
Branch N. C. Section – 1st Lt. J. R. Potts (c.112) 2/12N; 2/6SB
Crenshaw Va. Section – Cpt. Wm. Crenshaw/1st Lt. James Ellett (c.82) 2/10P; 2/12H; 2/6SB
Fredericksburg Va. Artillery – 1st Lt. Edward A. Marye (79) 2/10P; 2/12N
Johnson's Va. Section – 1st Lt. Valentine J. Clutter (88) 2/3R; 2/12H
Letcher Va. Btty. – Cpt. G. Davidson (c.82) 1/3R; 2/12N; 1/6SB
Pee Dee S. C. Arty. – Cpt. D. G. McIntosh (c.70) 1/10P; 1/3R; 1/12H; 1/12N
Purcell Va. Btty. – Cpt. W. J. Pegram (c.94) 2/10P; 2/12N

D.H. HILL'S DIVISION
Maj.Gen. Daniel H. Hill (Reported strength: 10,164) Staff: 26

IVERSON'S BRIGADE
Brig.Gen. Alfred Iverson (c.1,854) Staff: 4
5th N. C. – Maj. William J. Hill (c.552)
12th N. C. – Col. Henry E. Coleman (c.339)
20th N. C. – Lt.Col. Nelson Slough (c.472)
23rd N. C. – Col. Daniel Christie (c.487)

RAMSEUR'S BRIGADE
Col. Byron Grimes (c.1,835) Staff: 4
2nd N. C. – Col. William P. Bynum (c.510)
4th N. C. – Col. Byron Grimes (c.465)
14th N. C. – Col. Risden T. Bennett (c.450)
30th N. C. – Col. Francis Marion Parker (c.406)

DOLES' BRIGADE
Brig.Gen. George Doles (c.2,344) Staff: 4
4th Ga. – Col. Philip Cook (c.498)
44th Ga. – Col. John B. Estes (c.486)
1st N. C. – Col. M.S. Stokes (576)
3rd N. C. – Col. W. L. DeRosset (780)

COLQUITT'S BRIGADE
Brig.Gen. Alfred H. Colquitt (c.2,528) Staff: 4
6th Ga. – Col. John T. Lofton (c.617)
23rd Ga. – Col. Emory F. Best (c.649)
27th Ga. – Col. Charles T. Zachary (c.657)
28th Ga. – Col. Tully Graybill (c.332)
13th Ala. – Col. Birkett D. Fry (c.269)

RODES' BRIGADE
Brig.Gen. Robert E. Rodes (c.2,509) Staff: 3
3rd Ala. – Col. Cullan A. Battle (c.510)
5th Ala. – Col. Josephus M. Hall (c.595)
6th Ala. – Col. John B. Gordon (c.546)
12th Ala. – Col. Samuel B. Pickens (419)
26th Ala. – Col. Edward A. O'Neal (c.436)

D.H. HILL'S DIVISIONAL ARTILLERY
Maj. H. P. Jones (c.505) Staff: 2
Jeff Davis Ala. Arty. – Cpt. J. W. Bondurant (c.91) 2/3R; 2/12H
Morris Va. Btty. – Cpt. Richard C. M. Page (c.127) 2/3R; 1/12H; 3/6SB

Fry's Orange Va. Btty. – Cpt. Chas. W. Fry (c.91) 1/3R; 1/12H; 3/6SB
King William Va. Arty. – Cpt. Thomas H. Carter (119) 1/10P; 2/12H; 2/6SB
Hardaway's Ala. Btty. – Cpt. R. A. Hardaway (75) 2/3R; 1/WG

RESERVE ARTILLERY
Brig.Gen. Wm. N. Pendleton (c.792)

BROWN'S BATTALION
Col. J. Thompson Brown (454)
Brooke's Va. Btty. – Cpt. James V. Brooke (c.61) 1 /12H; 1/WG, 2/6SB
Powhatan (Dance's) Va. Btty. – Cpt. James Dance (c.84) 1/24H; 2/12H
3rd Richmond Howitzers Va. (Smith's) Btty. – 1st Lt. James Utz (64) 2/10P; 2/12H
Salem Flying Arty. Va. Btty. – Cpt. Abraham Hupp (c.78) 2/12H; 2/6SB
Rockbridge Arty. – Cpt. Wm. T. Poague (c.94) 2/20P; 2/10P
2nd Richmond Howitzers Watson's Va. Btty. – Cpt. David Watson (c.66) 2/10P; 1/12H; 1/HR;

CUTTS (SUMTER) GA. BATTALION
Lt.Col. Allen S. Cutts (c.383)
Co. A/Sumter – Cpt. Hugh M. Ross (130) 2/12H; 1/12N
Co. B/Sumter – Cpt. Geo. M. Patterson (c.130) 3/12H; 3/6SB
Co. C/Sumter – Cpt. John Lane (124) 2/20P; 3/10P; 1/WG

NELSON'S BATTALION
Maj. William Nelson (NA)
Amherst Va. Btty. – Cpt. Thos. J. Kirkpatrick (c.105)
Fluvanna Va. Btty. – Cpt. John L. Massie (c.73) 2/12H; 4/6SB
Milledge's Ga. Btty. – Cpt. Joh Milledge Jr. (273) 1/10P; 3/3R; 1/HR; 1/JR
Ell's Conn. Btty. – 1st Lt. W. F. Anderson (NA) 2/30P
Hanover Va. Btty. – Cpt. Geo. W. Nelson (NA)

CAVALRY DIVISION
Maj.Gen. James Ewell Brown Stuart (Reported strength: 10,701) Staff: 30

1ST CAVALRY BRIGADE
Brig.Gen. Wade Hampton (c.1,505) Staff: 5
1st N. C. – Col. Laurence S. Baker (c.407)
Cobb's Legion Cavalry Bttn. (9 co.'s) – Lt.Col. P. M. B. Young (c.330)
1st S. C. – Col. J. L. Black (c.339)
2nd S. C. – Col. Matthew C. Butler (c.186)
Phillips' Legion (5 co.'s) – Lt.Col. Wm. W. Rich (238)

2ND CAVALRY BRIGADE
Brig.Gen. Fitzhugh Lee (c.1,611) Staff: 4
1st Va. – Col. James H. Drake (c.311)
2nd Va. – Col. Thos. H. Munford (c.387)
3rd Va. – Col. Thomas H. Owen (c.225)
4th Va. – Col. Williams C. Wickham (c.550)
5th Va. – Col. Thomas L. Rosser (c.156)

3RD CAVALRY BRIGADE
Brig.Gen. W.H.F. (Rooney) Lee (c.1,937) Staff: 4
2nd N. C. – Col. S. Williams (c.152)
9th Va. – Col.T. R. T. L. Beale (c.495)
10th Va. – Col. J. Lucius Davis (c.203)
13th Va. – Col. J. R. Chambliss (c.305)
15th Va. – Col. Wm. B. Ball (c.780)

HORSE ARTILLERY
Maj. John Pelham (c.550) Staff: 9
Stuart 1st Horse Artillery (Breathed's) Va. Btty. – Cpt. James Breathed (c.107) 4/3R
Ashby's Horse Artillery (Chew's) Va. Btty. – Cpt. R. P. Chew (c.99) 1/3R; 1/12H; 1/3.1BR
Hart's (Washington Light)S. C. Btty. – Cpt. J. F. Hart (c.107) 4/3R
Stuart's Horse Artillery (Henry's) 2nd Va. Btty. – Cpt. M. W. Henry (c.125) 2/3R; 2/12N
Moorman's Va. Btty. – Cpt. M. N. Moorman (c.112) 4/3R

4TH BRIGADE (IN SHENANDOAH VALLEY)
Brig.Gen. W. E. Jones
6th Va. – Col. John S. Greene
7th Va. – Col. R. H. Dulaney
12th Va. – Col. A. W. Harman
17th Va. Bttn. – Lt.Col. O. R. Funsten
White's Va. Btty. – Maj. E.V. White

The Lacy House (Chatham) is across the river from town. Sumner was ordered by Burnside to stay off the front lines, so he established his headquarters there, from which he had a front row seat. An old house, Washington once visited there.

OPENING MOVES

Wednesday 10–11 December 1862

From the start Burnside's troops assembled, but he needed pontoons to span the river. Lady Luck hamstrung him at every move. The pontoon boats were late. His army saw that where there had been few or no Confederates across the river in late November, gray-clad shapes now observed them from the opposite shore. Surprise and deception dribbled away daily. Now Burnside could only hope to keep Lee guessing as to where the attack would come.

Burnside planned to threaten Fredericksburg with a three-pronged attack from bridge sites known as the Upper, Middle, and Lower Crossings. The Upper Crossing consisted of two pontoon bridges spanning the river opposite the foot of Hawke Street, near the site of an old rope ferry. The Middle Crossing was a single bridge crossing at the lower end of Fredericksburg, near the site of the burnt-out railroad bridge across the Rappahannock. The Lower Crossing consisted of two pontoon bridges laid a mile south of the middle bridges. They touched the west bank near the mouth of Deep Run, close to Hamilton's Crossing. Major Ira Spaulding of the 50th N. Y. Engineers was responsible for construction of the upper bridges; 1st Lt. Michael H. McGrath of the 15th N. Y. Engineers, the middle; and 1st Lt. Charles E. Cross of the regular army engineers, the lower ones.

10 December 1862

The army would cross into Fredericksburg and sweep up from both Marye's Heights and Prospect Hill, going north to dislodge the Confederates. Sumner's Right Grand Division lay at Falmouth, occupying the heights and securing the right flank of Burnside's army. Once pontoons were laid, they would secure the town, and then take the heights. This constituted half Burnside's main thrust, as he elected not to use the fords north-northwest of the city because he felt this would telegraph his plans to Lee (unfortunately, his wagons, teamsters, and mules conveyed his plans anyway). Franklin taking lower Telegraph Road was the other half of his scheme.

Fredericksburg had grown along a plain above the river. Factories, warehouses, homes, and businesses dotted the waterfront and were plainly visible from the Union side. A burnt-out railroad bridge's piers broke the water, and sometimes curious Confederates would gather to watch Union pickets on the far shore. Southern pickets in town found hidey-holes in waterfront buildings and dug rifle pits.

Hooker's Center Grand Division was to form the center of Burnside's army, while providing reinforcements for the other two Grand Divisions. In Burnside's original plan General Franklin's Left Grand Division, which formed the left flank, was to break through the Confederates and confuse Lee by rolling up Jackson's position at Hamilton's Crossing. Afterwards Burnside would claim his plan had hinged on Franklin taking Telegraph Road south of the heights above town. Franklin's men would push north up the road to displace the Army of Northern Virginia while Sumner (hearing of the attack) then attacked Marye's Heights. Stationed three miles south and on the east side of the Rappahannock from Fredericksburg, Franklin's Grand Division would threaten the Confederate right at Hamilton's Crossing, possibly taking Prospect Hill, to flank Lee's line, while Sumner crossed the river and took the heights above the town. A decent plan, but it depended on speed, superior numbers, and surprise. Delayed bridges had negated speed, and Burnside's presence was known, which ruled out surprise, so the only card Burnside had to play was superior numbers. Military conventional wisdom said that to take the heights by frontal assault the attacker needed a minimum of three times the number of defending troops.

Burnside had about twice as many troops as Lee, but their confidence in their commanders was low. To not attack might be fatal for the army's low morale because the Army of the Potomac spoiled for a fight. Attacking would give them a chance to win, to abort would be to admit defeat without even trying, perhaps sending the men erroneous messages about their fighting ability – and that might be worse than defeat.

Having seen the heights and hearing of Burnside's plan, Colonel P. C. Hawkins of the 9th New York said, 'If you make the attack as contemplated, it will be the greatest slaughter of the war; there isn't enough infantry in our whole army to carry those heights if they are well defended'.

Burnside shrugged off Hawkins' comment, saying, 'I expect to cross and occupy the hills before Lee can bring anything serious to meet me'.

Thursday 11 December – a Toehold on Town

Lee was ready for Burnside. Just where the push would come, he was uncertain, but he positioned troops to shift them along Telegraph road and the new military road to strengthen any areas threatened.

Longstreet's Corps held the heights. Jackson's Corps formed on Longstreet's right and extended the Confederate position down the chain of hills almost to the Massaponax.

Anderson's division protected the north side of Fredericksburg, from Stansbury Hill down to the Orange Plank Road. Ransom's division covered Marye's Heights where the Sunken Road lay concealed behind the famous stone wall. Ransom protected Anderson's right flank by extending the Confederate line south to Hazel Run. McLaws' division butted against Ransom's right flank and followed the high ground south from Hazel Run to Howison's Hill. A

Major General Daniel P. Woodbury was in charge of engineers, and thus of the building of the pontoon bridges at all crossing sites. Under his command at Fredericksburg were the 15th and 50th New York Engineers, as well as the regular army engineers.

Because bridges connecting the banks had been destroyed early in the war and not rebuilt, every time the Union chose to cross the Rappahannock at Fredericksburg, they had to establish pontoon bridges. These engineers built bridges for Sedgwick to cross four months after Fredericksburg in the struggle for Chancellorsville.

Taken in mid-December 1862 after the battle, this picture shows the Middle Crossing and Brown Island from the west bank, slightly to the south edge of town. Note the pilings rising from the waters. The high ground at the left behind the town is part of Marye's Heights.

detachment of Barksdale's men were on the town's waterfront to warn of a Federal Crossing. Barksdale's Mississippians covered those crossings from positions in houses, warehouses, and rifle pits along the riverbank.

South of McLaws' units at Howison's Hill, Pickett's division stretched to the northern shore of Deep Run, a narrow but deep creek slowed north-south movement. Pickett's men were primarily occupying the high ground west of the RF&P rail line. Hood held the high ground south of Deep Run, between Pickett on his left and A. P. Hill on his right flank. Hood's men held the area near Hamilton's Crossing, just south of where the Lower Crossing was planned. A. P. Hill's line extended from Hood's right flank south to Guinea Station. In front of Hill was an area between Archer and Lane's units where Gregg's brigade was pulled back because Hill thought the ground to Gregg's front was impassable. Stuart occupied the ground north of Guinea Station and east of the hills near Hamilton's Crossing.

Laying the Bridges

Burnside's plan came together – albeit late. Other commanders might have abandoned the attempt, but Burnside felt that although the element of surprise was gone, he could still bring Lee into battle and, force him west and away from Richmond. His plan moved ahead despite the fact that the Confederates knew of it.

Longstreet wanted to be ready for whatever happened so he sent reinforcements into Fredericksburg. At 0400 hours Thursday morning,

General Burnside and his staff met before the battle to discuss how to co-ordinate the attacks. He planned for Franklin to carry the southern heights, and when his men broke through, they would move north up Telegraph Road, where they would link up with Sumner's troops who had broken through at Marye's Heights, the combined actions forcing Lee to withdraw west.

FREDERICKSBURG

POSITIONS ON 10 DECEMBER 1862

General Hooker's Center Grand Division rests around 4 miles south of Stafford Court House and moves south-southwest toward Fredericksburg where it will form the centre of Burnside's army while providing reinforcements for the other two Grand Divisions.

General Sumner's Right Grand Division lies northwest of Falmouth nearly 2 miles from Fredericksburg, occupying the heights and securing the flank of Burnside's army. They are to cross the pontoon bridges and secure the town then take the heights above the city.

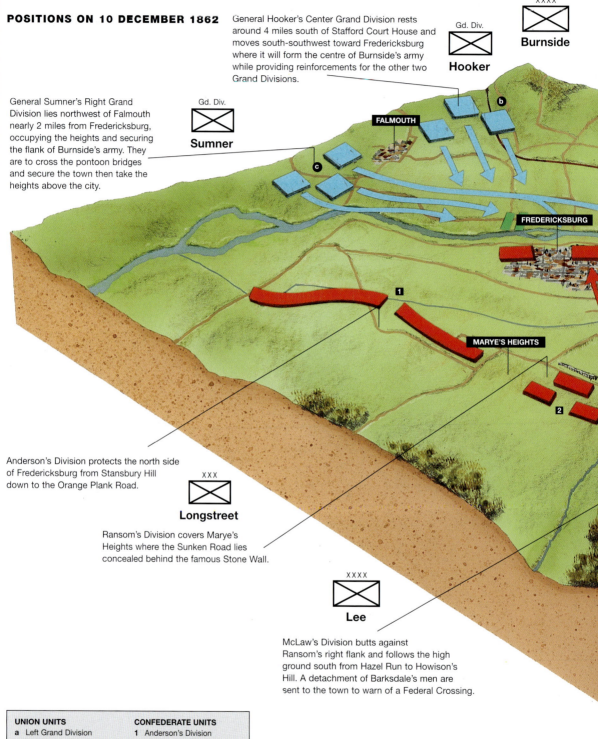

XXXX
Burnside

Gd. Div.
Hooker

Gd. Div.
Sumner

FALMOUTH

FREDERICKSBURG

MARYE'S HEIGHTS

Anderson's Division protects the north side of Fredericksburg from Stansbury Hill down to the Orange Plank Road.

XXX
Longstreet

Ransom's Division covers Marye's Heights where the Sunken Road lies concealed behind the famous Stone Wall.

XXXX
Lee

McLaw's Division butts against Ransom's right flank and follows the high ground south from Hazel Run to Howison's Hill. A detachment of Barksdale's men are sent to the town to warn of a Federal Crossing.

UNION UNITS	CONFEDERATE UNITS
a Left Grand Division	**1** Anderson's Division
b Center Grand Division	**2** Ransom's Division
c Right Grand Division	**3** McLaws Division
	4 Pickett's Division
	5 Hood's Division
	6 The Light Division (A. P. Hill)

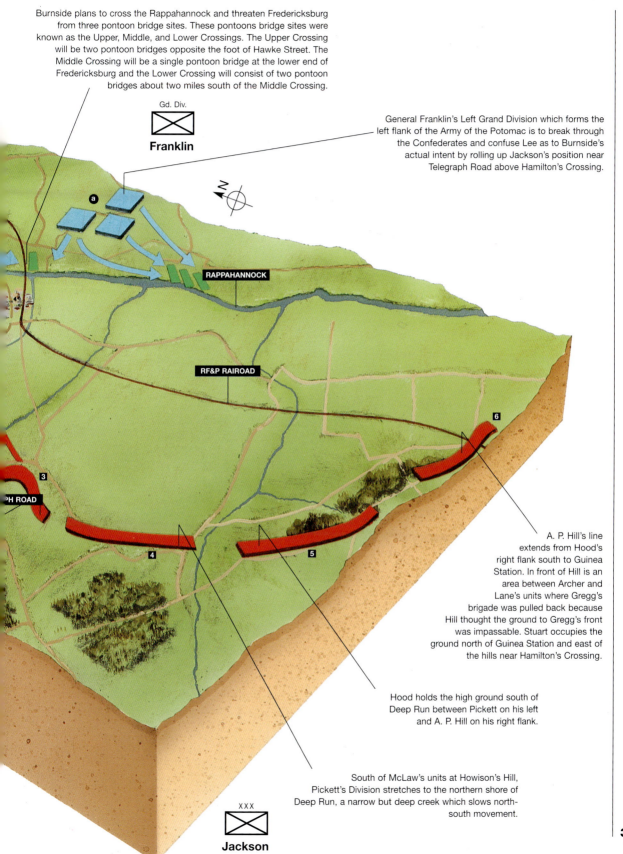

Burnside plans to cross the Rappahannock and threaten Fredericksburg from three pontoon bridge sites. These pontoons bridge sites were known as the Upper, Middle, and Lower Crossings. The Upper Crossing will be two pontoon bridges opposite the foot of Hawke Street. The Middle Crossing will be a single pontoon bridge at the lower end of Fredericksburg and the Lower Crossing will consist of two pontoon bridges about two miles south of the Middle Crossing.

Gd. Div.

Franklin

General Franklin's Left Grand Division which forms the left flank of the Army of the Potomac is to break through the Confederates and confuse Lee as to Burnside's actual intent by rolling up Jackson's position near Telegraph Road above Hamilton's Crossing.

RAPPAHANNOCK

RF&P RAIROAD

ᴾH ROAD

A. P. Hill's line extends from Hood's right flank south to Guinea Station. In front of Hill is an area between Archer and Lane's units where Gregg's brigade was pulled back because Hill thought the ground to Gregg's front was impassable. Stuart occupies the ground north of Guinea Station and east of the hills near Hamilton's Crossing.

Hood holds the high ground south of Deep Run between Pickett on his left and A. P. Hill on his right flank.

South of McLaw's units at Howison's Hill, Pickett's Division stretches to the northern shore of Deep Run, a narrow but deep creek which slows north-south movement.

xxx

Jackson

11 December 1862, four more elements of Colonel John C. Fiser's 17th Mississippi occupied the waterfront on the east side of Water (Sophia) Street, near the site of an old rope-drawn ferry. Captain Andrew J. Pulliam commanded the men from the 17th Mississippi north of Hawke Street, in preparation for the Union assault.

A young officer, Lt. Francis Seeley of Battery K, 4th US Artillery recounted the crossing on 11 December in his report:

'At five o'clock am December 11, the enemy's sharpshooters, from the houses on the south bank of the river, opened a vigorous fire on our engineers engaged in constructing the bridge, and compelled them to abandon their work.

'In compliance with your instructions, I immediately opened fire on the buildings, as did several others, and, after firing some 25 rounds of solid shot, succeeded in quelling temporarily the fire of the sharpshooters, but found it quite impossible to drive them from the buildings, as the cellars underneath afforded a secure refuge from our shots.

'About 12pm, I received orders from you to keep up a constant fire on the city, with which I complied, firing one round every five minutes, until 5pm, when, in compliance with orders from Major Doull, of General Hunt's staff, I opened a rapid fire, to protect the crossing of a small party of our own infantry, sent over to clear the cellars of the enemy's riflemen, which I continued about ten minutes, when, our infantry having reached the opposite bank, I ceased firing, having expended during the day 130 rounds of shrapnel and shot'.

In the early hours of the morning of 11 December 1862, Union pontoniers of the 50th N. Y. Engineers started ed assembling the bridges, bringing components down to

From the Confederate side of the river, looking at Union positions opposite Fredericksburg, earthworks and trenches in the foreground erected as breastworks were to defend against Union riflemen and artillery. Note the pilings from the burnt bridge breaking the water.

As seen from Chatham, opposite Brown Island, the bridge pilings are to the right, just about where the pontoon bridge for the Upper Crossing would be laid. Note the proximity of structures to the water's edge, and the trees lining Marye's Heights in the background.

the water's edge, with creaking wagons, braying mules, and much muttering from disgruntled mule-drivers – a sound which carried over darkened waters to the ears of the 17th Mississippi. Hearing the commotion, the Mississippians alerted McLaws that the Union army was coming across. At 0500 hours McLaws ordered two guns fired as a signal for Confederate troops to begin massing on the high ground west of Fredericksburg and Marye's Heights in preparation for a Union assault. Already the watch in town was being reinforced, as Barksdale moved his men forward.

At 0500 hours, at Market House, Barksdale set up his headquarters and retained half of the 21st Mississippi under Colonel Humphreys, while he ordered the remainder to Caroline Street to reinforce Lt.Col. William Luse's 18th Mississippi. About the same time, troops of the 8th Florida, under Captain William Baya, reinforced the Mississippians near the dock. They formed on the flank of Captain Andrew R. Govan's company of the 17th Mississippi south of the Middle Crossing, where the 15th New York Engineers were getting started.

In the growing light, Confederate pickets fired across the river at shadowy shapes and into the noisy dark masses at both the Upper and Middle crossing sites. At first the Union bridge layers moved ahead, but as the light improved, so did the Confederates' aim. When a shot was fired, everyone dashed for cover; after a while, the men returned to their work. Confederate fire steadily increased, until finally the Union engineers were driven away from the bridgehead. A few Southern riflemen held the Army of the Potomac at bay because no one wanted to risk his life to lay the bridge which would get them all across the river.

Union skirmishers from the 7th Michigan and 19th Massachusetts moved into position along the riverbank with Plumer's Massachusetts Sharpshooters, often shooting at the smoke which indicated a Confederate soldier's position.

Union commanders complained to Generals Woodbury and Hunt that their men were being exposed needlessly to Southern riflemen. The sniping was so effective that Union commanders' demands for help called down a Union barrage on the suspected Confederate positions. Using artillery to ferret out snipers was like using a shovel to swat flies. Still, the artillery fire was so intense that Southerners and citizens who had not fled could not leave their positions for water and were forced to suffer the ravages of thirst while hundred weights of shells shattered the masonry about them.

The Union barrage on Fredericksburg lasted until just after 1400 hours. When it ended, Confederates resumed their sniping en masse. They delayed the crossing for eight hours at the upper and middle sites.

A completed pontoon bridge has planks laid cross the punts (boats) and is anchored at both ends. To hold down sway and shifting because of currents, ties were often laid across planks to help steady the structure. Bridges such as these were used by Sumner's and Franklin's men crossing from the east to the west bank, and by Franklin for his route of withdrawal.

Earlier, at 0500 hours, the remainder of the 8th Florida, under Captain David Lang, moved into position on the north side of Pitt Street and east of Princess Anne Street to discourage any Union flankers who might find their way across. Throughout the morning they had little to occupy themselves except keeping their heads down during the Union artillery barrage. Around 1200 hours a near miss buried Lang under some rubble and his men dug him out. He was shaken and dizzy, though not seriously wounded, but his men refused to take part in the continued defense of the town.

Union Engineers attempted to lay the pontoon bridges under withering fire from Confederate snipers. Union skirmishers attempted to return fire, but with little effect. the crossing of the Rappahannock was delayed for over eight hours by the efforts of the Confederates.

By 0600 hours Humphreys' 21st Mississippi occupied houses and structures south of George Street and on the west side of Princess Anne Street as reserves to bolster Southern lines in case of a Union assault. At the same time Colonel James W. Carter's 13th Mississippi secured the area west of Princess Anne Street and north of Hawke Street, and then awaited further orders. They were to hold fast until needed.

The Bridgehead

Unable to put the upper and middle bridges across because of continuous Confederate harassing fire, Colonel Norman Hall of 3rd Brigade asked Lt.Col. Henry Baxter of the 7th Michigan if he would take some men across the river in punts and conduct an assault to chase away the riflemen and stop their harassing fire. Three units (the 7th Michigan, 19th Massachusetts, and 89th New York) from Hall's 3rd Brigade crossed in boats. Their mission: to drive the Confederates out of their positions. Lt.Col. Baxter led the 7th Michigan. Southern rifle fire on the storming force stopped two-thirds of the way across as the high river bank masked Confederate small arms fire unless the Mississippians wished to expose themselves. During the crossing Baxter was seriously wounded and Major Hunt assumed command of the assaulting force.

By 1430 hours on 11 December Major Thomas Hunt's 7th Michigan had landed at the foot of Hawke Street, formed a skirmish line, and, after a brief firefight, occupied a position along a crest of the embankment on the waterfront's south side at, Hawke Street and east of Water (present-day Sophia) Street. The 7th Michigan held fast and returned rifle fire, which kept sniper fire at the pontoniers across the river at a minimum in their sector. When the 19th Massachusetts arrived, at nearly 1500 hours, followed about a quarter of an hour later by the 20th Massachusetts, the 7th Michigan assaulted the positions along Water Street and captured 31 Southerners in 20 minutes of fierce fighting.

At 1515 hours a cross-section of volunteers from Colonel Harrison Fairchild's 89th New York landed near the Middle Crossing and engaged the 17th Mississippi and Baya's 8th Florida when they attempted to occupy warehouses south of the railroad tracks and west of Water (Sophia) Street.

By 1450 hours the 19th Massachusetts had landed and assumed positions north of Hawke and east of Water (Sophia) Street. The

Union engineers selected the possible sites for the pontoon bridge crossings, and then they realized that Southern soldiers, gathered across the river at a mill dock in Fredericksburg, were intently watching them in the relatively calm days before the assault.

combined 7th Michigan and 19th Massachusetts moved inland from the bridgehead to force elements of the 17th Mississippi to withdraw from houses along Water (Sophia) Street and reposition west one block, to houses along Caroline Street, fighting a withdrawing action house to house. Union troops then occupied houses and firing positions vacated by the withdrawing Confederates.

The soldiers from Michigan and Massachusetts captured prisoners and created a small beach-head at the water's edge along Water Street. Major Macy of the 20th Massachusetts was supposed to have crossed as soon as the bridge was completed, but either through impetuousness or misunderstanding orders, he put his men into punts and crossed, landing just about the time the bridge reached the far shore at 1520 hours. Their arrival made the bridge-head too crowded and forced the 7th Michigan and 19th Massachusetts to expand further into town to make room for them, capturing 31 Confederates in the ensuing firefight and close combat.

When the 7th Michigan assaulted, around 1530 hours, the 17th Mississippi fell back, withdrawing to houses along Caroline Street. Once there, they laid down covering fire when men of the 7th Michigan attempted to close; their firepower and accuracy was so great that the Union assault stalled.

Around 1530 hours the 21st Mississippi, under Major Daniel N. Moody, dug in south of the train tracks and east of the train depot near Lt.Col. Luse's 18th Mississippi, to stop Union troops from the dock (the 89th N.Y.) from taking any more ground. But the die had been cast, because both Upper and Middle crossings could now be used.

Men had to move inland or die, because successive waves of troops had no place to go if the attack stalled. Slowly Union soldiers spread along the waterfront, fighting their way into occupied buildings as Southerners withdrew. Soon the Union controlled Water Street's eastern side and the water's edge, but still they had to venture further inland.

Federal troops battled to push Southerners out of Fredericksburg so Sumner could funnel troops into the city for the assault on Marye's Heights the following day. South of the city, at the Lower Crossing where Franklin waited, bridge-heads were secured and bridges thrown across by regular US Army Engineers, who finished the job at 1230 hours.

On Thursday 11 December 1862, between 1600 and 1700 hours, as the fighting intensified at the south end of Fredericksburg with the 89th New York, Cpt. Baya's group of the 8th Floridians declared they were leaving; later the 18th Mississippi and elements of the 21st Mississippi decided to pull back under cover of increasing twilight, thinking the Floridians had already left. The

Another view of the mill in Fredericksburg, seen from the Middle Crossing site. Note how close to the water's edge were the mill and other buildings which would later house Confederate sharpshooters.

Mississippians' withdrawal cut off the 8th Florida, who did not pull out when they said they would. As a result, many were captured by the 89th New York, who then remained stationary in dockside buildings, protecting the middle bridgehead for further use.

At the north end of the city remnants of Lang's command as well as the battered 17th Mississippi withdrew and angled toward Marye's Heights, careful to move from one covered position to another while enough light remained for Union artillerists to identify and fire on them. The 13th Mississippi arrived to replace them.

A view today from the Union side of the Rappahannock looking upriver at Fredericksburg in spring. Foliage obscures all but the church spire, still standing nearly a century and a half later. In winter most of the trees are bare. The wide river is deep enough to prevent fording near the city, and in winter ice extends up to ten feet from either bank toward the center.

Fight for the Bridgehead

The 19th Massachusetts held buildings on the right side of Hawke Street at the bridgehead and the 7th Michigan held those on the left. The 20th Massachusetts arrived and lined up in the shelter of the river bank. Shortly afterwards the 42nd New York, 59th New York, and 127th Pennsylvania crossed to the western shore and outskirts of Fredericksburg to deploy along the waterfront.

Colonel Hall ordered Major Hunt of the 7th Michigan and Captain Weymouth of the 19th Massachusetts to deploy one street south of their original position. Acting as skirmishers for the advance of the 19th Massachusetts, the 7th Michigan stalled when it ran into renewed rifle fire near the corner of Fauquier Street and Water Street. On either side of Fauquier Street they found shelter from Confederate sniper fire which came from houses, basements, backyards, and behind fences. The 20th Massachusetts was supposed to pass by them to the secure buildings, but in crossing Water Street at Fauquier Street they drew heavy rifle fire, whereupon Colonel Hall ordered Macy and Abbott to execute a right face and in a column of fours move west up Fauquier to clear out Confederate riflemen.

Barksdale sent elements of the beleaguered 21st Mississippi along Princess Anne Street to bolster the 13th Mississippi's right flank, and he sent the rest to Water Street to slow up the Union advance. The 106th Pennsylvania led the Union advance south along Water Street toward the junction of Water Street and William Street, supported by the 72nd Pennsylvania and 42nd New York.

Meanwhile the 7th Michigan was to provide skirmishers, but under the close-range Southern rifle fire they sought refuge in an alley. 'No man could live beyond that corner', Hunt argued from his alley. Both Macy and Abbott of the 20th tried to rally the men of the 7th Michigan and they appealed to Major Hunt, but the Midwesterners would not leave their shelter, though Macy chided them for two to three minutes as his stationary unit sustained severe damage. Realizing that they would

ACTION AT THE BRIDGEHEAD, 11 DECEMBER 1862

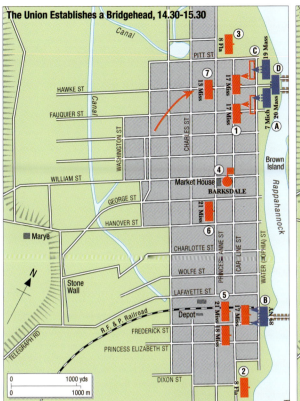

The Union Establishes a Bridgehead, 14.30-15.30

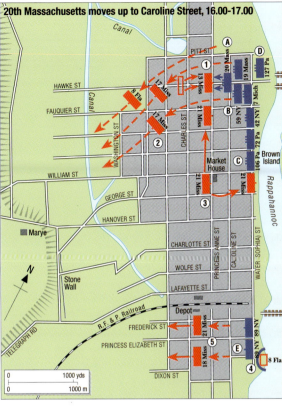

20th Massachusetts moves up to Caroline Street, 16.00-17.00

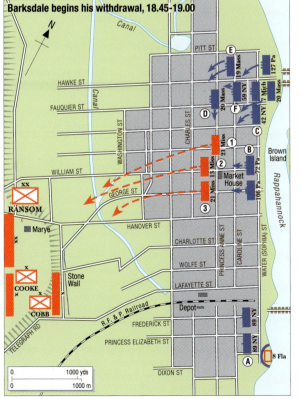

Barksdale begins his withdrawal, 18.45-19.00

The Union Establishes a Bridgehead, 1430-1530

A. 1430 hours, the 7th Michigan under Maj. Thomas Hunt lands at the foot of Hawke Street.
B. 1515 hours, Col. Harrison Fairchild's 89th New York lands near the middle crossing.
C. 1450 hours, the 19th Massachusetts lands at the foot of Hawke Street.
D. 1520 hours, the 20th Massachusetts took the punts across the Rappahannock.
1. 0400 hours, elements of Col. John C. Fiser's 17th Mississippi occupy the waterfront.
2. 0500 hours, troops of the 8th Florida form on the flank off the 17th Mississippi.
3. 0500 hours, the remainder of the 8th Florida is positioned to the north side of Pitt Street.
4. 0500, Barksdale sets up his headquarters at Market House.
5. 1530 hours, the 21st Mississippi digs in south of the train tracks and east of the depot.
6. 0600 hours, the 21st Mississippi occupies houses and structures south of George Street.
7. 0600 hours, the 13th Mississippi secures the area west of Princess Anne Street.

20th Massachusetts moves up to Caroline Street, 1600-1700

1. The 13th Mississippi arrives to take its place in the line,
2. The remnants of Lang's element of the 8th Florida as well as the 17th Mississippi withdraw.
3. Barksdale sends elements of the beleaguered 21st Mississippi along Princess Anne Street.
4. The 8th Florida are cut off and many are captured by the 89th New York
5. The 18th Mississippi and elements of the 21st Mississippi withdraw as the fighting intensifies.
A. The 20th Massachusetts arrives to relieve the 19th Massachusetts and the 7th Michigan.
B. The 59th New York, 7th Michigan and 19th Massachusetts occupy the area of Hawke Street.
C. The Union column advances south along Water Street, led by the 106th Pennsylvania.
D. The 127th Pennsylvania arrives across the upper bridge to guard the bridgehead.
E. After capturing a contingent of the 8th Florida, the 89th new York remained stationary.

Barksdale begins his withdrawal, 1845-1900

A. At the south end of town, where the 89th New York holds the middle crossing, fighting has virtually stopped.
B. The 72nd and 106th Pennsylvania continue west turning down William and George streets respectively.
C. The 42nd New York, 7th Michigan and half the 20th Massachusetts force their way south and southwest
D. Elements of Cpt. Macy's 20th Massachusetts move forward and attack.
E. The 19th Massachusetts supports this attack.
F. The 59th New York is caught in fierce house to house fighting.
1. The 21st Mississippi slow the union advance through their sniping
2. The 13th Mississippi falls back down Princess Anne Street
3. Elements of the 21st Mississippi follow them

not budge, Macy cursed, 'To hell with your unit!' and told the 20th Massachusetts to clear the way. He left the Midwesterners in the alleyway and followed his command. The 20th Massachusetts passed by the mauled 19th Massachusetts and 7th Michigan to advance westward down Hawke Street, where fierce building to building fighting ensued. Union soldiers with fixed bayonets forced their way deeper into town. Macy went forward, leaving the 7th Michigan behind. Reaching Caroline Street, the 20th came under intensified fire from both sides of the street and from the portion of Fauquier Street due west of them.

Major Macy deployed Company I to face west, up Fauquier Street, and turned Company A to face north on Caroline and Company K to face south, thus forming three sides of a hollow square. Ahead and in buildings along both Lewis Street and Hawke Streets elements of the 21st Mississippi fired into the Union formation. In some cases Union soldiers were within feet of the Southern riflemen's concealed positions. Men of the 20th Massachusetts were shoulder to shoulder, four abreast, as they advanced down Fauquier Street. Soldiers from companies C, D, and G came to fill in as others fell to Southern fusillades. Bodies lay everywhere.

Abbott took Company I into a house to the left of Fauquier and west of Caroline to shelter them from fire coming from further up the street. He intended to force his way from house to house west on Fauquier and dislodge the Confederate riflemen ahead of them.

The 59th New York, 7th Michigan (now rallied), and 19th Massachusetts followed the 20th Massachusetts to occupy the area of Hawke Street between Water Street and Caroline Street. The 127th Pennsylvania crossed the Upper bridge to town, where they guarded the bridgehead even as strong resistance from the newly arrived 13th Mississippi threatened to force the Union troops off their northernmost toehold in Fredericksburg. Company K of the 20th Massachusetts held fast, although most of its men were down or wounded. They did not fall back, and when relieved by the 59th New York, only eight men were fit for duty.

As night fell, fire first slackened and then ceased. As the 59th New York moved up, remnants of the 20th Massachusetts withdrew with their wounded to the riverbank. They had lost 113 of 335 effectives, about one-third of their strength, but their persistence had forced Barksdale's men back.

Until now Barksdale had held the town, fearing that if he withdrew in daylight, Union artillery would savage his retreating troops. At the south

end, where the 89th New York held the Middle Crossing, fighting had stopped. Barksdale began to give ground, first withdrawing the 17th and 18th Mississippi.

The 72nd and 106th Pennsylvania advanced, turning west down William Street and George Street respectively. The 42nd New York, 7th Michigan, and half the 20th Massachusetts forced their way west and southwest, while elements of the 21st Mississippi made the Union troops move cautiously for fear of snipers. Gradually the 13th Mississippi, with elements of the 21st Mississippi, fell back along Princess Anne Street. The 59th New York was embroiled in fierce fighting down an alley which ran parallel to Water Street and Caroline Street between Fauquier and Pitt. The 19th Massachusetts supported the 20th Massachusetts in an attack along Princess Anne Street.

As night became absolute, Barksdale ordered all his remaining troops to withdraw, leaving the 21st to act as rearguard. Gradually fire slackened, as the Confederates left town and found their way between units on Marye's Heights to re-form at the rear. Fredericksburg had fallen to the Army of the Potomac.

MARYE'S HEIGHTS

12–13 DECEMBER 1862

To the west of Fredericksburg rose Marye's (pronounced Marie's) Heights. A stone wall bordered the east side of a sunken road, making excellent cover, with a firing step formed by the east bank of the road. A line of firing positions and rifle pits extended from the wall toward the woods north of town.

In front of the stone wall ran a rail fence, and slightly downhill, nearer town, the ground dipped in a slight depression. Massed Confederate artillery could not all fit in line behind the infantry, so part of it was positioned to bring enfilading fire on attackers. Replacements and reinforcements stood ready, so if Burnside broke through, Longstreet could plug the line with Ransom's and Kershaw's brigades. Down the incline from the stone wall was the slight depression; beyond that, a mill race, and then the town, with its distinctive spires reaching skyward.

Throughout the day Lee and Longstreet watched the Union troop build-up. Lee knew the massed men would come at Longstreet's line, at Marye's Heights. He asked 'Old Pete' Longstreet if he was worried. Longstreet looked at town, then studied his positions, the emplacements, the kill zone in front of the wall, and where his men were waiting. There could be no defense better than the one he had prepared. Confederate artillery commander Colonel E. Porter Alexander had assured him that not only small arms, but also artillery fire would saturate the grounds leading up to the heights, saying 'General, we can cover that ground... so well that we comb it as with a fine-tooth comb. A chicken could not live on that field when we open [fire] on it'. Old Pete was ready, come what may.

As seen from the Lacy House, this Union battery faces west, commanding the city of Fredericksburg. It is one of the best period photos showing Union artillery batteries, caissons, and gunners ready for action.

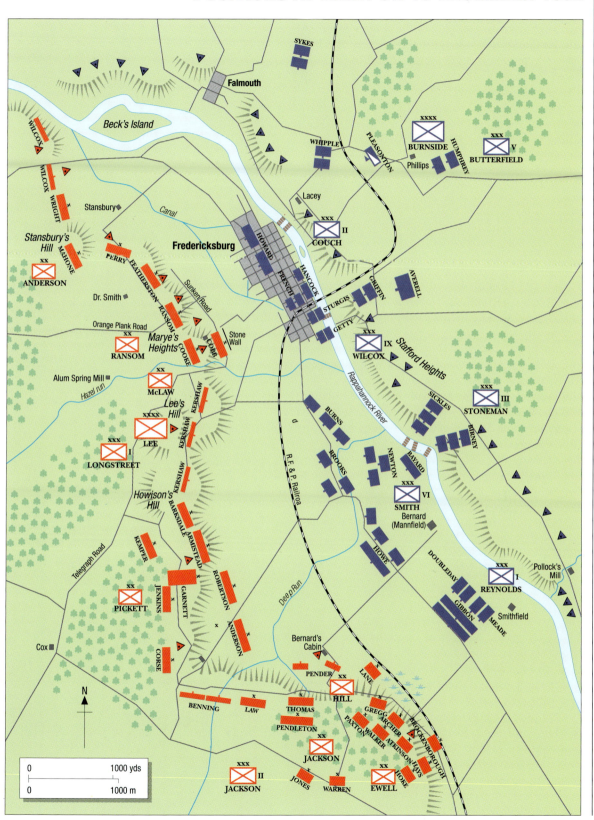

SYKES

Falmouth

Beck's Island

WILCOX

WILCOX

WRIGHT

Stansbury

Canal

Fredericksburg

Stansbury's
Hill

MAHONE

PERRY

FEATHERSTON

ANDERSON

Dr. Smith

Sunken Road

RANSOM

Orange Plank Road

RANSOM

COOKE

Marye's
Heights

COBB

Stone
Wall

Alum Spring Mill

McLAW

KERSHAW

Hazel run

Lee's
Hill

KERSHAW

LEE

LONGSTREET

KERSHAW

BARKSDALE

ARMISTEAD

Howison's
Hill

KEMPER

ROBERTSON

Telegraph Road

GARNETT

JENKINS

PICKETT

ANDERSON

Cox

CORSE

N

BENNING

LAW

PENDLETON

THOMAS

PENDER

LANE

HILL

WHIPPLE

PLEASONTON

Phillips

BURNSIDE

HUMPHREY

XXXX

XXX

BUTTERFIELD

V

Lacey

COUCH

XXX

II

HOWARD

FRENCH

HANCOCK

STURGIS

GRIFFIN

AVERELL

GETTY

WILCOX

XXX

IX

Stafford Heights

Rappahannock River

SICKLES

STONEMAN

XXX

III

BIRNEY

BURNS

BROOKS

NEWTON

BAYARD

SMITH

VI

XXX

Bernard
(Mannfield)

R.F. & P. Railroad

HOWE

DOUBLEDAY

REYNOLDS

XXX

I

Pollock's
Mill

Smithfield

GIBBON

MEADE

Deep Run

Bernard's
Cabin

GREGG

ARCHER

PAXTON

WALKER

ATKINSON

BROCKENBOROUGH

HAYS

JACKSON

XX

JACKSON

XXX

II

JONES

WARREN

HORE

EWELL

XX

47

The defense of Marye's Heights' section fell to Brig.Gen. Thomas R. R. Cobb's Georgians, who waited behind the stone wall. Cobb's position was supported by General Cooke's command and Ransom's men plus the Washington Louisiana Artillery. Throughout the days of 11 and 12 December they sat and waited, huddling together for warmth in the frosty evening; finally they saw the distant, dim sun rise while they drank chicory and waited still.

Once Barksdale's men had left the city, Burnside moved as many troops as possible into town, men bedded down in the road along Caroline and Water Street, huddling for warmth and often stripping wooden doors, furniture and shutters from homes for kindling. There they stayed throughout the long day of 12 December, careful to keep a low profile lest their activity bring on a Confederate artillery barrage.

More than six divisions and their support units overflowed the streets and banks east of Fredericksburg by noon the next day. Whereas the house to house fighting and street combat of the day before had limited Union expansion, the city was now empty of Confederates. As the day dragged on, Union soldiers foraged in the deserted houses, some with their roofs missing and others with only two or three walls remaining upright, but all empty. Other houses had been damaged with shot and shell like victims of gigantic boring beetles, and some few homes were untouched.

Most residents of Fredericksburg had abandoned town. Many feared the coming of the Yankees, and apprehension galloped rampant. Homes stood empty and lines of citizens carrying paltry belongings or driving wagons overstuffed with their few movable worldly goods sought refuge with neighbors who lived safely away from town.

Some homes and dwellings were intact, their furnishings left in place. The refugees could not carry anything except their most precious possessions, and the town was open for the taking. Slaves were sometimes abandoned in the confusion, and many were left in the wake of the fleeing Southerners, fending for themselves as best they could, hoping that the Union troops would treat them kindly.

Dawn saw fog rising from the river. A ghost town lay where days before a thriving city had been. Burnside had given orders forbidding looting, but Union troops stuffed knapsacks, pockets, and pillowcases. What they didn't steal, they destroyed, often burning furniture in makeshift bonfires to warm themselves in the damp of the evening below the twinkling fires of Confederates watching from Marye's Heights.

Provost guards on the bridges stopped looters and relieved them of their bounty, but they only salvaged the most obvious booty: rugs, huge paintings, massive silver services, and the odd chair. Looting was not confined to the ranks, and some officers were seen with expensive furnishings. What was hidden from the provost guards' eyes went undetected, and between the shelling, fleeing populace, and rapacious

Mississippian William Barksdale was told to take his regiment, notify Longstreet of a Union crossing, and then slow up the Union advance through town. Fighting from warehouses, cellars, rifle pits, and street corners, the men from Mississippi held up Sumner from just after dawn until after dark in the nearly deserted town.

In February the Philips House caught fire, and this shows Hooker's men at the ruins, after trying unsuccessfully to quell the flames.

Burnside made the Phillips House his headquarters. After the plans on 13 December went awry, he decided to lead an assault by IX Corps on 14 December 1862. His commanders met with him here and convinced him that such an assault would fail more miserably than the previous ones. Burnside relented and the scheduled assault was canceled.

Northerners, Fredericksburg was picked clean.

Some bonfires roared out of control, and houses were soon ablaze. Among the Union soldiers, some were firemen in more peaceful times, including much of the 72nd Pennsylvania, and they threw themselves at the blazes along Caroline Street, attempting to save what little they could; still when dawn came, more than one home was a smoldering pile of embers. The fine town was tattered, much of it in ruins, and one Federal soldier lamented, 'It made me sad to think how comfortable the homes were in time of peace, now turned into desolation'.

General Franklin put a third pontoon bridge across the Rappahannock on 12 December. Not as stable as the earlier two, this bridge was suitable for infantry crossing only; still, it enabled Franklin to cross his troops in two-thirds of the time it would have otherwise taken.

Late afternoon Burnside met with Franklin, Smith, and Reynolds to discuss the thrust of the following day. At dawn Franklin was to seize the military road by breaking through Jackson's line and rolling up the Confederate flank. Burnside left the meeting, assuring Franklin that orders would come at once, but he did not write them immediately upon his return to headquarters. The orders only reached Franklin around 0730 hours 13 December, having been written about 0555 hours and sent by Chief of Staff J. G. Parker. By the time they arrived, the sun was up and the element of surprise had vanished.

Franklin's orders read: 'Keep your whole command in position for a rapid movement down the Old Richmond Road, and you will send out

Confederate small arms fire was so devastating that Union generals asked for an artillery barrage on town to attempt to drive the Southern marksmen away. In one of the heaviest barrages of the war which lasted nearly two hours, Fredericksburg was shelled time and again, with little effect on the dug-in Confederates but with great damage to homes.

at once a division at least to pass below Smithfield, to seize, if possible, the height near Captain Hamilton's, on this side of the Massaponax, taking care to keep it well supported and its line of retreat open. He [Burnside] has ordered another column of a division or more to be moved from General Sumner's command up the Plank Road to its intersection with the Telegraph Road, where they will divide, with a view to seizing the heights on both of these roads. Holding these two heights, with the heights near Captain Hamilton's, will, he hopes, compel the enemy to evacuate the whole ridge between these points. He makes these moves by columns distant from each other, with a view of avoiding the possibility of a collision of our own forces, which might occur in a general movement during a fog. Two of General Hooker's divisions are in your rear, at the bridges, and will remain there as supports. Copies of instructions given to Generals Sumner and Hooker will be forwarded to you by an orderly very soon. You will keep your whole command in readiness to move at once, as soon as the fog lifts. The watchword... will be "Scott"'. Through a misunderstanding, Franklin believed his attack was to continue only if it was apt to succeed, hinging mostly on the words 'if possible'.

Sumner's orders dated 13 December, 0600 hours were more specific: 'Extend the left of your command to Deep Run, connecting with General Franklin, extending your right as far as your judgment may dictate. He [Burnside] also directs that you push a column of a division or more along the Plank and Telegraph Roads with a view to seizing the heights in the rear of the town. The latter movements should be well covered by skirmishers, and supported so as to keep its line of retreat open. Copy of instructions given to General Franklin will be sent to you very soon. You will please await them at your present headquarters, where he (the general commanding) will meet you'. The orders continued, 'Great care should be taken to prevent a collision of our own forces during the fog. The watchword... will be "Scott". The column for a movement up the Telegraph and Plank Roads will be got in readiness to move, but will not move till the general commanding communicates with you'.

Watchful Confederates waited on Marye's Heights. It was a killing ground prepared for the Yankees, and the soldiers in blue were getting ready to walk straight into the sights of the waiting Confederates. Riflemen at the sunken road stood behind the stone wall as protected as if in a fortress with a firing step. Porter's semi-prophetic words seemed to hang in the air,: 'A chicken could not live on that field when we open fire on it'.

Some houses were blown up, others lost roofs or walls. Some appear almost unharmed except for the round holes left by solid shot, giving them the appearance of having been attacked by gigantic boring beetles. Judging from the entry holes, this house faces east. Exit holes are larger and more ragged

On Willis' Hill, near Marye's Heights, houses came under bombardment. This one brick home was virtually knocked down by the hundredweights of shells which hit it. Others in town suffered a similar fate. When the shelling ceased, Confederates crawled from holes and cellars to resume sniping at Union engineers trying to assemble the pontoon bridges.

Lee watched the gathering of blue-clad soldiers. He said to Longstreet, 'They ... will break your lines, I am afraid'.

Longstreet, a little amused at Lee's concern, replyed, 'General, if you put every man on the other side of the Potomac on that field to approach me over the same line, and give me... plenty of ammunition, I will kill them all before they reach my line. Look... right; you are in some danger there'. Then he added, 'But not on my line'.

Sumner understood that his assault depended upon Franklin's success, and he readied his men. When Franklin did not easily push through, Sumner was ordered around 1100 hours to advance his troops. General Couch received a telegram telling him to start his advance. He ordered General French to take Telegraph Road, supported by Hancock's division, while Howard's division was to go up the Plank Road at his order.

The fog was impenetrable. It had arrived during the night and stayed, making the early morning sun a faint butter-stain on gray clouds which were a continuation of the fog, so that the demarcation between land and sky was anyone's guess. Sound carried, distorted. Although a curse to the spy, it was a boon to the soldier for the fog was a harbinger of warmer weather. Observers could see no more than 250 yards, so both armies had relatively hidden movement. It was eerie, hearing vast numbers of men move but not being able to see them. Around 1000 hours the fog burned off.

Burnside readied the Army of the Potomac. Hooker remained in reserve, while Franklin attacked the Confederate right flank near Hamilton's Crossroads. If he could break the Confederate line, he could march north on Telegraph Road and make Marye's Heights untenable, dislodging the Southerners. Sumner's Grand Division was to assault Marye's Height head-on. The military road extension of Telegraph Road behind the stone wall would allow Lee to send units to reinforce Cobb's Georgians, who held the crucial length of hilltop. Burnside had planned no real flanking or supplemental attack other than Franklin's thrust, which meant that Sumner's assault faced the brunt of Confederate firepower if Franklin didn't come through.

Lee's men held the high ground behind the city and to the south as well as flanking both wings of Burnside's army. Confederate artillery would hit attacking Union troops from every side but the rear. Any Union initiatives on Marye's Heights had to be uphill across a murderous field of fire.

Cobb's men were positioned at the wall. As a precaution, Cooke's men were positioned behind them, but once the Union intent was clear, Southern soldiers would stand there more than three ranks deep.

Were one superstitious, one might have found a way to avoid attacking on 13 December, but evidently Burnside was not; still, it might have been better if he had been. Units were on the move as early as 0500. As of 0800 everyone was in position.

SUMNER'S SIX ASSAULTS

Six divisions would assault in successive waves, and when one broke through, the others would follow to carry the Confederate position. Burnside and his commanders did not realize how many of its defensive features were hidden from view until the Union troops were within a couple of hundred yards; by then it was too late. An unimaginative man, Burnside had little subtlety, and felt that a head-on approach would carry the day because of his superior numbers. He did not realize that although the attacker may have superior numbers to the troops defending any one portion of a line, those defenders were aided by enfilade fire, volley fire, fortified positioning, and ready reinforcements. The Union attacks were ill-advised from the start, and sheer madness as they progressed, re-enacting the same scenario time and again.

Union troops gathered in the dubious shelter of the city streets. As soon as it was light a Southern artillery barrage hit buildings and streets, exploding masonry and cobblestones, which did nearly as much damage as direct hits. In tight-packed units, the men could only move forward.

Major General Edwin Vose Sumner was Burnside's oldest commander, and his most loyal Grand Division leader. A member of the 'old' army, Sumner wanted to command from the front and accomplish his mission to take Marye's Heights. Unfortunately, Burnside denied him the former; Lee, the latter.

THE FIRST ASSAULT: 1200–1300 HOURS

Brigadier General William H. French's division (3rd Division, II Corps) was the first to assault the stone wall held by Cobb's Georgians and the 24th North Carolina. They massed along Princess Anne Street between Wolfe Street and Charlotte Street. Hancock's division (1st Division, II Corps) followed, ready. Howard supported French's right flank, Getty's and Sturgis' men, his left. French's men were to assault in waves – Kimball's brigade then Andrews', with Palmer's following last.

On Marye's Heights Cobb was supported by nine guns from the Washington Louisiana Artillery, a veteran unit. Cooke's unit moved behind to support Cobb's position. When French's division advanced, the Confederates rose to fire en masse into the approaching Federal soldiers at less than 200 yards. Someone commented that with such a ferocious charge, no doubt the Union expected him to give up the stone wall. 'If they wait for me to fall back, they will wait a long time', Cobb replied.

Kimball's line shuddered when the volley hit. The next torrent of gunfire shattered their resolve. Andrews' men behind took up the slack, marching through the sundered remains of Kimball's brigade only to be bashed by a wall of lead which blunted their impetus. Palmer's brigade met a similar fate.

Time and again Southerners blasted holes into the blue ranks, which wavered, started, then wavered again. Continual volley fire drove the surviving Union soldiers back to the safety of the depression. Dead and wounded boys in blue dotted the ground between the lip of the depression and the wooden fences.

This photograph, taken just after the battle, shows the terrible destruction the town suffered. Union troops mustered in the deserted streets and prepared for their trek up Marye's Heights and Confederate artillerymen dropped shells into them before they reached their point of embarkation.

In General French's words: 'At 12pm I received orders to attack and the movement at once commenced. The heights to be carried were about three-quarters of a mile outside of the town, crowned by batteries with rifle-pits and walls beneath, forming a continuous line of defense. The skirmishers... debouched from the town rapidly... deploying as soon as they crossed the bridges of the canal at the railroad depot'. He continued: 'A heavy infantry and artillery fire was opened upon the line which, however, spread itself out over the plain. Kimball's brigade, moving by the left flank, followed immediately [by]... Colonel J. W. Andrews... followed [by]... Colonel Palmer.

'The column of attack was now complete, the head of which had not arrived in front of the enemy's rifle pits at short musket range. The skirmishers, having driven the enemy to cover, were met with a terrible fire on the front and flanks, and compelled to lie down, slightly protected by the undulations of the plain. The brigades, shattered by the fire to which they were exposed, filled up the serried lines of the 1st Brigade and poured their fire into every part where the enemy appeared... Still, the heads of the columns rushed on up to the very walls, melting away before superior numbers in strong positions. My troops now covered themselves to the right and left of the front of attack, opening a cross-fire upon it, with such execution as to slacken its fire.

'Hancock's division, following mine in order, and contending against the same difficulties, steadily came up. At my request, he re-enforced the part of my line of skirmishers which was holding the houses to the right and farthest to the front...' French ends with: 'My division was on the field four hours, and retired only when relieved by fresh troops'.

French's losses were 1,153 killed, wounded, or missing when his division retired from the field, leaving the dead, dying, wounded and stunned to make their way off as best they could.

Union commanders feared a counter-attack and a Union artillery barrage blasted Confederate positions while Hancock's men moved into position. During the barrage a piece of shrapnel hit General Thomas R. R. Cobb in the head. He fell seriously wounded, and was evacuated, dying en route to a field hospital from loss of blood. Shortly thereafter, General Cooke assumed command and was also wounded, whereupon General Kershaw took command at the stone wall.

Hancock's men were the second group to assault Marye's Heights. The Irish Brigade was one of his units, and although that crack unit moved as close to the stone wall as any Northern unit, they were stopped 30 yards from the wall by gunfire, ironically from troops of Irish descent.

THE SECOND ASSAULT: 1300 HOURS

Brigadier General Hancock's division assaulted Marye's Heights next. His men were not directly behind French's division, having moved toward his rear right flank. Brigadier General O. O. Howard's division spread itself along Hanover Street and George Street to minimize themselves as targets for Confederate artillery. Brigadier General Samuel Sturgis's division occupied an area near the train depot and Brigadier General Getty's division held the Union left flank in town. Remnants of French's division lay protected in a slight depression and could offer no support to Hancock in the second assault.

THE ASSAULTS ON MARYE'S HEIGHTS

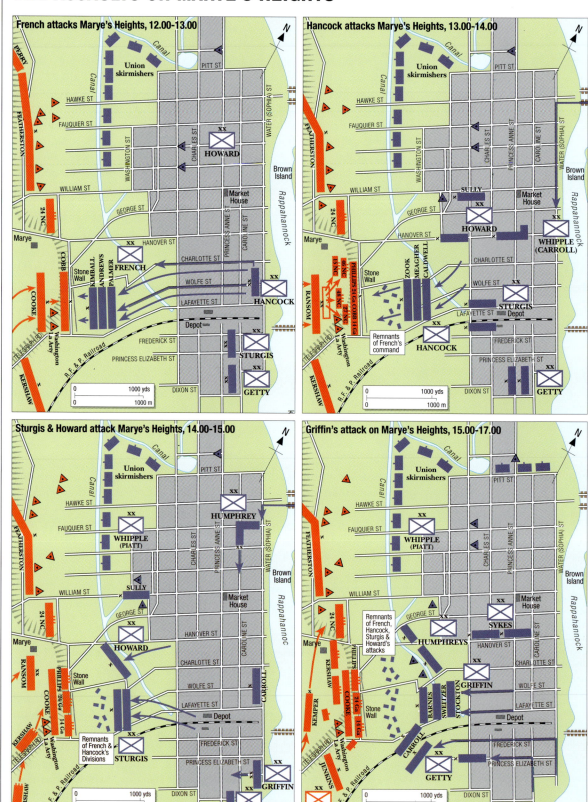

French attacks Marye's Heights, 12.00–13.00

Hancock attacks Marye's Heights, 13.00–14.00

Sturgis & Howard attack Marye's Heights, 14.00–15.00

Griffin's attack on Marye's Heights, 15.00–17.00

Meanwhile Cooke's men advanced and formed a second rank behind Cobb's men. Ransom brought his men forward as a third line. Brigades fired, stepped back and loaded while another brigade fired, and then moved forward to fire again while the other reloaded.

As the Union artillery barrage lifted, Hancock's men jumped to their feet and charged in waves. Colonel Samuel Zook's 3rd Brigade led, followed by Meagher's Irish Brigade (2nd Brigade), and Caldwell's 1st Brigade brought up the rear. Confederates held their fire until the Union soldiers were close, then a rippling wall of gunfire erupted. Zook's men were shattered.

Hancock said, 'Colonel Zook's brigade was the first in order. As soon as it had formed line, it advanced to the attack with spirit, passing the point at which the preceding troops had arrived, and being joined as it passed by the brave regiments of Kimball's brigade and some other regiments of French's division. It failed... to take the stone wall, although our dead were left within 25 paces of it. These troops still held their line of battle in front of the enemy and within close musketry range'.

THE ASSAULT OF THE IRISH BRIGADE

The Irish Brigade was the second wave of Hancock's Division to storm the stone wall. Keeping their greatcoats on, the men of the 116th Pennsylvania, 28th Massachusetts, 63rd, 69th, and 88th New York took off backpacks and other gear which would slow them down.

As the Irish Brigade moved out of Fredericksburg, Confederate artillery found their range. Even so, only a few fell or dropped out, even though more were wounded. In parade ground ranks they pressed forward.

General Meagher wanted the Confederates at the stone wall to realize they faced the men of the Irish Brigade. The regimental flags of the New Yorkers were so badly damaged by shot that all three had been returned to New York for replacement days earlier, and only the 28th Massachusetts had its color present, so they were placed in the middle of the formation. Then Meagher put a sprig of boxwood in his kepi so all would know who they faced. Officers of the Irish Brigade were all given sprigs of boxwood (the closest they could come to shamrocks) to give their men to wear in their kepis which would identify them as Irishmen – and so they went into battle wearing something green. The 28th Massachusetts carried its one-sided green regimental standard bearing the golden harp into battle. It bore the Gaelic motto 'Faugh A Ballagh' (Clear the way).

Many of Cobb's Georgians were of Irish descent, and although a worried and regretful murmur ran along their line, none stepped

Humphreys & Getty attack Marye's Heights, 17.00–18.00

away as their fellow Irishmen advanced, crossed the canal, and moved toward the wall where they waited. 'What a pity, here comes Meagher's fellows', muttered Irish voices in Cobb's line. The Confederate line left to right had the 24th North Carolina at a far northern section of wall, a gap in the wall, then Phillips' Georgia legion, the 24th Georgia, and the 18th Georgia along the stone wall proper. Behind them left to right were the 46th North Carolina between the 24th Georgia and Phillips' legion, and the 27th North Carolina to the rear and slightly left of the 18th Georgia. Further behind, the 15th North Carolina waited near the Marye House and on a line with them but behind and between the 27th North Carolina and 46th North Carolina. The 48th North Carolina waited to see where it would be needed. The 2nd South Carolina moved up near the line and the South Carolina Palmetto Guard took a position south along Hazel Run to defend the flanks. Kershaw's remaining units fanned out on line with the 3rd and 7th South Carolina nearest the Marye House.

The Irish Brigade moved through town in regimental columns led by the 69th New York, followed in sequence by the 88th New York, 28th Massachusetts, 63rd New York, and finally the 116th Pennsylvania. Behind the ridge at the base of the hill they assumed a line two ranks deep, with the 69th on the left and the 116th on the right. Seeing their determined stride, Captain Thomas Galloway of the 8th Ohio observed how resolved they were to take the wall or die trying, 'Every man has a sprig of green in his cap and a half-laughing, half-murderous look in his eyes'.

Stopping at the base of the hill to regroup and dress their line, they were sheltered from the worst effects of the fire. Ahead they could see the survivors and the dead of French's division.

Meagher's brigade approached to less than a hundred yards on the 'double quick'. The Union line left to right was the 116th Pennsylvania, the 63rd New York, the 28th Massachusetts in the center with its colors flying, the 88th New York, and on the far right the 69th New York. They advanced through the depression, stepping around the dead and wounded but keeping their formation. Resolute, their weapons ready, they advanced to the wooden fence. Suddenly Cobb's men stood and unleashed a staggering volley, which reeled the line as it closed to within 150-200 yards of the stone wall. Canister raked them, leaving huge gaps in the formation. Men of the Irish Brigade fell as they had advanced – in orderly rows. They reached within 75 yards of the wall when a blast of withering fire decimated their ranks so that bodies fell row upon row. Try as they might, they could not close with the wall. Survivors bent forward as if struggling into the face of a fearful nor'easter as they moved through the hail of lead. When they reached the wooden fence, another volley rippled through their ranks, knocking down what seemed to be every third man. Wounded and staggering, Adjutant J. R. Young and Major William Horgan of the 88th made it nearly 30 yards further before collapsing.

In the 116th, Sgt. Tyrell carried the colors. Wounded in the leg, he fell to his knees, standard upright. Five shots shook him as they hit, and another shattered the flagstaff, making him drop the colors. Tyrell fell.

General Thomas R. R. Cobb's Georgians were the men who held the wall. Behind them Cooke's men gathered to form a brigade second rank, and even further back, Ransom waited. He was killed by shrapnel on Marye's Heights, from where he could see the house in which his mother had been born.

Then the 116th's survivors fell back, seeking any shelter from the rain of death. Realizing the colors were left at the wooden fence, Lt. Quinlan left the shelter of the ditch, ran back to where Tyrell lay and rescued them. Returning, he ran, stumbled, and rolled to the ditch as Confederate fire erupted the ground around him. Tyrell later recovered, despite multiple wounds.

The Irish Brigade tried to recover its momentum and take the wall but subsequent volleys sent them reeling. So valiant were their efforts that a strange thing ensued: Confederates, who also shot at them, cheered their bravery! Thirty yards from the stone wall the brigade ground to a halt and its survivors returned a volley. Then, after another murderous Southern volley, they began to withdraw in small groups.

Meagher's report summed up their actions. 'On Saturday the 13th... we were ordered under arms... at 8am. The column moved up the street, headed by Col. Robert Nugent and his veteran regiment, being exposed during the march to a continuous fire of shot and shell, several men falling from the effects of each. Even while I was addressing the Sixty-ninth, which was on the right of the brigade, three men of the Sixty-third were knocked over, and before I had spoken the last word of encouragement the mangled remains – mere masses of blood and rags – were borne along the line.

'Advancing up the street we crossed the mill-race ... the first defense of the enemy. The entire brigade, consisting of 1,200 men, had to cross a single bridge, and passing to the right, deploy into line of battle. This movement necessarily took some time to execute. The Sixty-ninth going on the right, was compelled to stand its ground until the rest of the brigade came up and formed. This ordeal it had to endure for fully half an hour.

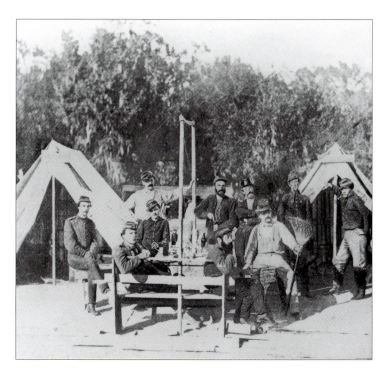

Men of the Washington Louisiana Artillery waited behind Cobb (slightly right, rear) with eight guns. The remainder of their unit poured enfilade fire into advancing Union soldiers, while those behind Cobb fired directly into the advancing lines of assault troops – with deadly results.

'I directed Colonel Nugent to throw out two companies of his regiment as skirmishers on the right flank. I had hardly done so before the Eighty-eighth, Sixty-third, Twenty-eighth, and One hundred and sixteenth, coming up, and deploying themselves in line of battle, drew down upon the brigade a still more terrific fire. The line, however, was beautifully and rapidly formed, and then boldly advanced, Colonel Nugent leading the Sixty-ninth on the right, Col. Patrick Kelly, commanding the Eighty-eighth ... [and] ... Maj. Joseph O'Neill, commanding the Sixty-third.

'The center was assigned by me to the Twenty-eighth Massachusetts Volunteers, commanded by Col. R. Byrnes (this regiment carrying the only green flag this day). On the left

The 28th Massachusetts (shown here with their regimental banner) held the centre of the Irish Brigade's line. They marched up the hill in close order, leaning into the hail of bullets that greeted them from the Confederate positions along the stone wall.

of the line was the One hundred and sixteenth Pennsylvania Volunteers, a new regiment; it had but very recently joined the brigade, but ... it has proved itself worthy of the cause into which with so much enthusiasm it had thrown itself.

'Thus formed, under unabating tempest of shot and shell, the Irish Brigade advanced at the double-quick against the rifle-pits, the breast-works, and batteries of the enemy...'.

By nightfall the survivors had found their way back to Union lines. Of nearly 1,200 men, 545 were wounded, killed or missing. Of these, the 69th New York lost almost half its complement. In assaulting their objective and failing, they charged into history.

Caldwell's men were not to be stopped. They charged, but were slapped down by canister and small arms fire. They suffered a similar fate to rest of Hancock's division.

Hancock noted in his report, 'The Irish Brigade next advanced to the assault. The same gallantry was displayed, but with the same results. Caldwell's brigade was next ordered into action, and, although it behaved with the utmost valor, failed to carry the enemy's position. All the troops then formed one line of battle, extending from a point... to the right of Hanover Street, in a line nearly parallel to the enemy, with the left thrown back, the extreme left extending about the front of two regiments to the left of the railroad culvert. This line... held the entire day and until relieved... some... regiments not coming off the field until 10 o'clock the following morning'.

Confederate fire was devastating. Hancock's shattered men fell back to join French's troops in the depression. Dead and injured dotted the ground between the depression and an area 50 yards in front of the stone wall, forming an additional obstacle for future attacking troops. Hancock's losses were 2,032 men killed, wounded and missing.

THE THIRD ASSAULT: 1400 HOURS

General Sturgis' and General Howard's units were to attack Marye's Heights in tandem. Trying to hit the stone wall with two groups from two different directions at once, Sturgis' men surged forward from their positions by the railroad depot and Howard's men approached on an angle from the area between Charlotte Street and Hanover Street. Both were raked by enfilading fire.

Sturgis later stated, 'I moved my division at once to the upper portion of the city. Toward the front, sheltering the troops as much as possible from the fire of the enemy under cover of the fences, houses, etc... General Couch now commenced the attack, but the fire of the enemy's artillery and musketry was so severe that his left was soon broken and rolled back in irregular masses toward the city.

'Observing this disaster, I ordered General Ferrero (12.30pm) to advance with four regiments of his brigade, leaving the fifth... to support Dickenson's battery. Under cover of the battery, General Ferrero now moved forward... completely checking the advance of the foe and forcing him back with heavy loss. As soon as Lt. Dickenson's battery opened, the enemy concentrated a very heavy artillery fire upon it, and I was forced... to withdraw it.

'I sent forward the 1st Brigade under General Nagle, with order to take his position on the left of Ferrero... to open a cross-fire'. Nagle couldn't negotiate the terrain and so

General Joseph Hooker would later meet failure in the area at Chancellorsville, but during this battle he went to Burnside and asked him to stop the assaults which were proving to be little more than the senseless slaughter of Union soldiers. Burnside refused and ordered the attacks to continue.

After the battle of Chancellorsville, in April 1863, when this photo was taken, the Confederates broke. But in 1862 this wall and sunken road provided a natural firing parapet for Southerners, who poured sheets of rifle fire into the advancing Union brigades, shattering them and foiling Burnside's plan to run off the Confederates and take Richmond.

Sturgis had him and the 51st N. Y. move by another route to support the 2nd Brigade. 'Every man fought as if the fate of the day depended upon his own individual exertion. They fought... until every cartridge was expended... [and remained]... until regularly relieved at 7.20pm by the division of General Griffin'.

On the Southern line Ransom's men moved slightly to the left rear of Cooke's men, covering the gap between Cobb's men and the 24th North Carolina. Kershaw's men moved behind Cooke's troops. Combined with artillery fire, the Confederate rifles threw down a wall of lead accompanied by a sheet of flame every time they fired. Again the Union attack was stopped cold by volley fire. Survivors sought refuge where remnants of French's and Hancock's divisions huddled. Gradually survivors were winding their way back to Union lines, careful to keep their heads down and moving in ones or twos, as the slightest movement seemed to draw wrathful Southern fire.

Brig.Gen. O. O. Howard's men were to attack the works to Hancock's right. Col. Joshua T. Owen's 2nd Brigade led the way across the mill race and, upon reaching a ploughed field to the left, deploy into a line of battle and advance. Howard noted, 'He [Owen] moved... to the vicinity of a small brick house, where he halted, ... and ... caused the men to lie down within 100 yards of the enemy's first line. I sent him word to hold what he had got, and to push forward at the first opportunity, and not to fire, except when he had something to fire at. Colonel Hall... was ordered... to deploy to the right of Hanover Street. He made several attempts to storm the enemy's right positions, but the concentrated fire of artillery and infantry was too much to carry the men through... I held General Scully in the outskirts of the town, ready to support or relieve either brigade. Colonel Hall sent for reinforcements, stating that his ammunition was getting low. General Sully sent him two regiments which prolonged his line to the right.

'This... was the condition of things at 4pm: Owen extending from the road; Hall extending from the same road to the right. Now a brigade of General Humphreys'... formed in my rear'. As Humphreys' units charged the stone wall, they passed Howard's line, and 'a portion passed it a little, met a tremendous volley of musketry and grape, and fell back. One of my regiments, the One Hundred and Twenty-Seventh Pennsylvania, went with him. All were rallied at the mill-race ravine.

'After several ineffectual attempts to carry the enemy's works, darkness came on and the firing subsided. My division remained out to the front and was not withdrawn until relieved by Generals Sykes, Hall, and Sully, about 12'.

THE IRISH BRIGADE STORMS THE STONE WALL

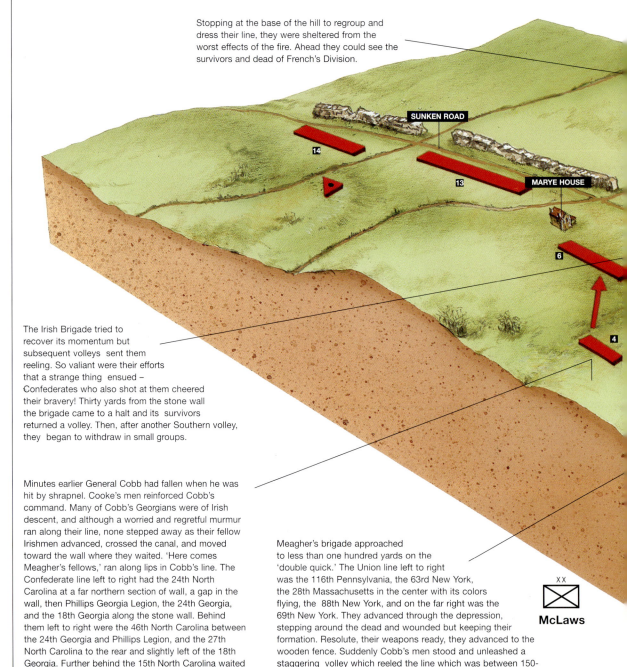

Stopping at the base of the hill to regroup and dress their line, they were sheltered from the worst effects of the fire. Ahead they could see the survivors and dead of French's Division.

SUNKEN ROAD

14

13

MARYE HOUSE

6

4

The Irish Brigade tried to recover its momentum but subsequent volleys sent them reeling. So valiant were their efforts that a strange thing ensued – Confederates who also shot at them cheered their bravery! Thirty yards from the stone wall the brigade came to a halt and its survivors returned a volley. Then, after another Southern volley, they began to withdraw in small groups.

Minutes earlier General Cobb had fallen when he was hit by shrapnel. Cooke's men reinforced Cobb's command. Many of Cobb's Georgians were of Irish descent, and although a worried and regretful murmur ran along their line, none stepped away as their fellow Irishmen advanced, crossed the canal, and moved toward the wall where they waited. 'Here comes Meagher's fellows,' ran along lips in Cobb's line. The Confederate line left to right had the 24th North Carolina at a far northern section of wall, a gap in the wall, then Phillips Georgia Legion, the 24th Georgia, and the 18th Georgia along the stone wall. Behind them left to right were the 46th North Carolina between the 24th Georgia and Phillips Legion, and the 27th North Carolina to the rear and slightly left of the 18th Georgia. Further behind the 15th North Carolina waited near the Marye House and on a line with them but behind and between the 27th North Carolina and 46th North Carolina the 48th North Carolina waited to see where it would be needed. The 2nd South Carolina moved up near the line and the South Carolina Palmetto Guard took a position south along Hazel Run to defend the flanks. Kershaw's remaining units fanned out on line with the 3rd and 7th South Carolina nearest the Marye House.

Meagher's brigade approached to less than one hundred yards on the 'double quick.' The Union line left to right was the 116th Pennsylvania, the 63rd New York, the 28th Massachusetts in the center with its colors flying, the 88th New York, and on the far right was the 69th New York. They advanced through the depression, stepping around the dead and wounded but keeping their formation. Resolute, their weapons ready, they advanced to the wooden fence. Suddenly Cobb's men stood and unleashed a staggering volley which reeled the line which was between 150-200 yards from the stone wall. Canister from artillery raked them, leaving huge gaps in the formation. Men of the Irish Brigade fell as they had advanced, in orderly rows. Survivors bent forward as if struggling into the face of a fearful nor'easter as they moved through the hail of lead. When they reached the wooden fence, another volley rippled through their ranks, knocking down what seemed to be every third man. Wounded and staggering, Adjutant J. R. Young and Major William Horgan of the 88th made it nearly 30 yards further before collapsing.

X X
⊠
McLaws

X X X
⊠
Longstreet

General Meagher wanted the Confederates at the stone wall to realize they faced the men of the Irish Brigade. The regimental flags of the New Yorkers were so badly damaged by shot that all three had been returned to New York for replacement, and only the 28th Massachusetts had its color present, so they were placed in the middle of the formation. Then Meagher put a spring of boxwood in his kepi so all would know who they faced. Officers of the Irish Brigade were all given springs of boxwood to give all their men to wear in their kepis (the closest they could come to shamrocks) which would identify them as Irishmen – and so they went into battle wearing something green. Only the 28th Massachusetts carried its one-sided green regimental standard with the golden harp on it into battle with them. It bore the Gaelic motto, 'Faugh A Ballagh' (Clear The Way).

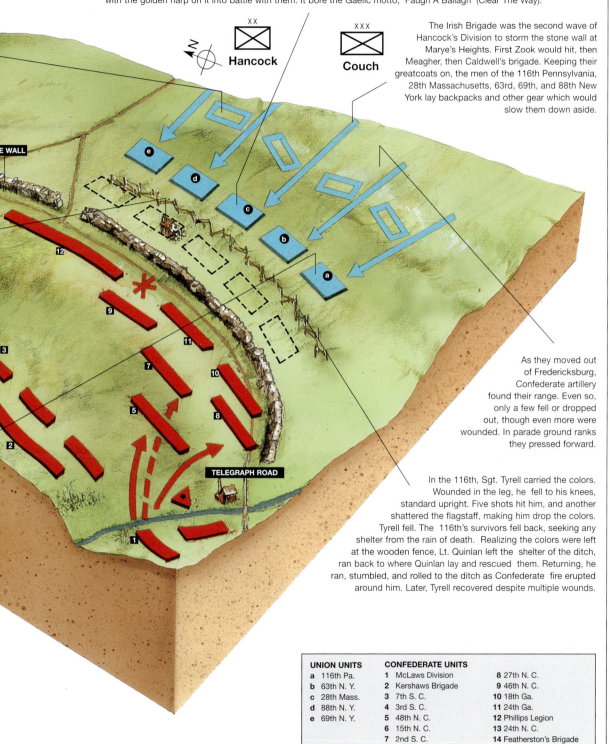

Hancock

Couch

E WALL

TELEGRAPH ROAD

The Irish Brigade was the second wave of Hancock's Division to storm the stone wall at Marye's Heights. First Zook would hit, then Meagher, then Caldwell's brigade. Keeping their greatcoats on, the men of the 116th Pennsylvania, 28th Massachusetts, 63rd, 69th, and 88th New York lay backpacks and other gear which would slow them down aside.

As they moved out of Fredericksburg, Confederate artillery found their range. Even so, only a few fell or dropped out, though even more were wounded. In parade ground ranks they pressed forward.

In the 116th, Sgt. Tyrell carried the colors. Wounded in the leg, he fell to his knees, standard upright. Five shots hit him, and another shattered the flagstaff, making him drop the colors. Tyrell fell. The 116th's survivors fell back, seeking any shelter from the rain of death. Realizing the colors were left at the wooden fence, Lt. Quinlan left the shelter of the ditch, ran back to where Quinlan lay and rescued them. Returning, he ran, stumbled, and rolled to the ditch as Confederate fire erupted around him. Later, Tyrell recovered despite multiple wounds.

UNION UNITS	CONFEDERATE UNITS	
a 116th Pa.	1 McLaws Division	8 27th N. C.
b 63th N. Y.	2 Kershaws Brigade	9 46th N. C.
c 28th Mass.	3 7th S. C.	10 18th Ga.
d 88th N. Y.	4 3rd S. C.	11 24th Ga.
e 69th N. Y.	5 48th N. C.	12 Phillips Legion
	6 15th N. C.	13 24th N. C.
	7 2nd S. C.	14 Featherston's Brigade

Sturgis' 2nd Division lost 1,002 men killed, wounded, or missing; Howard, 914 men. Still the lines of Union troops trudged forward to try and take the stone wall.

After watching the carnage of the first attempts, Hooker studied the ground, and convinced that another attack was doomed to failure, rode back to find Burnside. When he found Burnside, he urged him to countermand his orders for further attacks. Burnside replied that the heights had to be taken that very afternoon – and his orders would stand. The attacks would continue.

Hooker left Burnside and rode back to his headquarters. It was not easy to tell his commanders they marched their men into almost certain death, but he explained that Burnside's response had been dogmatic: Griffin, then Sykes, and finally Humphreys would try to carry the stone wall.

THE FOURTH ASSAULT: 1500 HOURS

The Confederates realized how fiercely this battle was being waged. Ransom's men held just west of Marye's Heights while Kemper put units in front of the Marye House and behind the 24th North Carolina. Jenkins moved north of the railroad to support Cobb's right flank.

Brig.Gen. Charles Griffin had waited since 0500 hours for his chance. At 1300 hours his division was ordered across the river, and at 1400 hours they massed in the streets of Fredericksburg. At 1500 hours Butterfield ordered Griffin to support Sturgis' command and take the heights if feasible. At 1530 he was ordered to relieve Ferrero's men.

No finesse, no subtlety, no feints: Griffin sent his division straight at the wall. Barnes' brigade took the lead, followed by Sweitzer; Stockton's brigade brought up the rear.

Confederate offensive fire did not slacken, and its force drove Union soldiers back a few steps. Supporting Griffin's attack were Humphreys' men to his right and Carroll's men, backed by part of Getty's command, to his left.

Col. J. B. Sweitzer led 2nd Brigade forward. Confederate fire had not diminished. His men fell as wheat before a thresher. Soon they were mingled with the survivors of earlier waves, hugging the ground and praying for darkness which would alleviate the accuracy of the Southerners' fire. As Griffin noted in his report, 'Our troops advanced, exposed to a severe enfilading fire from both directions, and from a direct fire of artillery and musketry in front. Our lines moved up to within a few yards of the enemy's infantry, who were pro-

Taken in 1861, this picture of Michigan infantry shows uniforms which were influenced by French-Canadian woodsmen and European armies. Each man carried not only a rifle, but a revolver of choice. Rifles were topped with the socket bayonet.

Major General Darius Couch's II Corps received the brunt of the assaults against the stone wall. Hancock, Howard, and French were his division commanders. These assaults so badly mauled II Corps that when Burnside proposed a second day of assaults, he chose IX Corps.

tected behind stone walls and in trenches, when the fire became so galling that they were compelled to fall back behind the crest of a knoll.

'The division occupied their ground... until about 10pm... when it was relieved'. He ends stating 'The loss of this division was 66 killed, 752 wounded'.

When Griffin's assault ended, the ground in front of the stone wall was covered with a mass of quivering, thrashing wounded and dead who had dropped in their tracks. The fourth assault had failed.

THE LAST ASSAULTS: 1700 HOURS

Artillery fire from the flanks as well as from the Washington Louisiana battery has been very effective. Massed rifle fire had shattered four earlier attempts. Confederate soldiers were standing back to belly nearly six ranks deep in places, waiting for the next assault. Daylight was almost gone.

Humphreys' division attacked uphill angling southwest. Getty's moved up along Frederick Street and Princess Elizabeth Street and crossed the RF&P railroad tracks to attack uphill, moving northwest in an attempt to avoid the murderous field of fire directly in front of the wall.

Humphreys later reported, 'My division... received orders at 2.30 in the afternoon to cross the river and enter Fredericksburg... I received an urgent request from Major General Couch to support that part of his corps on the left of the Telegraph Road. 2nd Brigade, commanded by Colonel Allabach... moved to the front, and ... 1st Brigade [was to] ... form on its right'.

He recalled the terrain as 'a ravine crossing the Telegraph road, where the troops could form under partial cover; then to the high ground above, on which, some 200 yards in advance of them was a heavy stone wall, a mile in length, which was strengthened by a trench. This stone wall was at the foot of the heights... the crest of which, running 400 yards distant from the wall, was crowned with batteries. The stone wall was heavily lined with the enemy's infantry'.

Thomas Meagher was the leader of the Irish Brigade. A colorful man who had escaped from transportation, he made his way to the United States, formed the 69th New York, which became the basis for the brigade, and later was appointed acting governor of Montana.

Humphreys' account continues: 'The 2nd Brigade ... moved rapidly and gallantly up to General Couch's troops, under the artillery and musketry fire of the enemy. The nature of the enemy's line of defense could not be clearly perceived by me until I reached our line. The troops I was to support, as well as those on their left... were sheltering themselves by lying on the ground'. His men had trouble getting forward because 'part only... were able to reach the front rank, owing to the numbers already occupying the ground. The continued presence of the troops I was to support or relieve proved a serious obstacle to my success. As soon as I ascertained the nature of the enemy's position, I was satisfied ... that the only mode of attacking him successfully was with the bayonet'. Humphreys commented next that his troops had been in service only four months and that getting them to stop firing and fix bayonets was a difficult chore. But through force of his personality he managed to convince them to cease firing, to fix their bayonets, and charge the stone wall.

65

'The charge was then made, but the deadly fire of musketry and artillery broke it, after an advance of 50 yards. Colonel Allabach re-formed the brigade, a portion in the line from which the charge was made, and the remainder in the ravine from which they had originally advanced'. Humphreys moved 2nd Brigade, but in the process received three orders from Butterfield and Hooker telling him the heights must be taken 'before night'. He managed to bring order to Tyler's men, and 'the bayonet alone was the weapon to fight with here. Anticipating, too, the serious obstacle they would meet with in the masses of men lying under the little shelter afforded by the natural embankment in front... who could not be got out of the way, I directed them to disregard these men entirely, and to pass over them'. Both he and Tyler led the brigade 'under the heaviest fire yet opened, which poured upon it from the moment it rose from the ravine'.

At the Fredericksburg visitor center today, a reconstructed stone wall on a slight rise lets visitors get the feel for what the six Union assault waves faced on that day in 1862. The actual stone wall was higher and bordered a sunken road. The sides of the road provided a firing step so an infantryman in the road was relatively safe from Union small arms fire.

Humphreys' account continues: 'As the brigade approached the masses of men... every effort was made by the latter to prevent our advance. They called to our men not to go forward, and some attempted to prevent by force their doing so. The effect upon my command was what I apprehended – the line was... disordered and... forced to form into a column, but still advanced rapidly. The fire of the enemy's musketry and artillery, furious as it was before, now became still hotter. The stone wall was a sheet of flame that enveloped the head and flanks of the column. Officers and men were falling rapidly, and the head of the columns was... brought to a stand when close up to the wall. Up to this time not a shot had been fired by the columns, but now some firing began. It lasted but a minute, when, in spite of all our efforts, the columns turned and began to retire slowly. I attempted to rally the brigade behind the natural embankment... but the united efforts of General Tyler, myself, our staffs, and the other officers could not arrest the retiring mass.

Humphreys communicated the result... to General Butterfield, and received directions in return to bring the remainder of my troops to the ravine. When it was over Humphreys' losses in both brigades were heavy – more than 1,000 killed and wounded, 'including in the number officers of high rank. The greater part of the loss occurred during the brief time they were charging and retiring, which scarcely occupied more than ten or fifteen minutes for each brigade.'

In conclusion he states, 'I cannot refrain from expressing the opinion that one of the greatest obstacles to my success was the mass of troops lying on our front line. They ought to have been withdrawn before mine advanced. The troops on their right and left would have prevented the enemy from advancing. Finding them lying there, the men of Allabach's brigade, who had never before been in battle, instinctively followed their example. Besides, they disordered my lines and were greatly in the way when I wished to bring the brigade to a charge... [They] not only impeded its progress, but converted it... into a massive column, too large to be managed properly'.

Humphreys' attack had been blunted by enemy fire and the mass of disorganized troops unable to withdraw because of Confederate fire. Hooker's last word on the charge shows how he felt about the attack in general: after he ordered the attack, he watched Humphreys' unit savaged by Confederate fire and then called off the attack because he had lost 'about as many men as he was ordered to sacrifice'. Later Burnside would have these words and others like them in mind when he issued General Order 8, mentioning Hooker foremost.

Brig.Gen. George Getty's 3rd Division, IX Corps, was the last Union hope as night fell. His men knew about the boiling cauldron of gunfire they to be were asked to walk into – and they knew that earlier attempts had failed. Getty's report reads: 'Early in the morning of December 13th, the division was moved to the extreme lower end of Fredericksburg, near Hazel Creek. While in that position, the troops suffered considerably by the premature bursting of shells from Diedrich's battery, First New York Artillery Battalion.

'At 5pm orders were received... commanding Ninth Army Corps to advance by brigade front and charge the enemy. Colonel Hawkins, 1st Brigade, was to advance by the right of companies, halt, and re-form behind the railroad, and then advance in line to the attack. Colonel Harland, 2nd Brigade, was to follow in similar formations and support Colonel Hawkins'. Seeing troops of another command in the lee of a ravine, Getty sent his staff officer to ask them to support his attack. At first no officer was found, but then a Major Byrnes agreed to do so. However, when the attack started, Byrnes 'failed to do this'.

Getty's line made it to within 50 yards of the wall before they received a thunderous volley which shattered their ranks. They attempted to rally, but fire was too intense. However, they had full knowledge of the previous failed attacks and theirs seemed but a half-hearted effort. As before, the Confederates slashed the approaching waves of Union soldiers with withering rifle and cannon fire.

In his after-action report, Getty claimed, '1st Brigade reached the railroad without any accident, and, forming behind it, advanced to the attack in tolerable order. But it was now dark, and after advancing well up to the enemy's line, the 1st Brigade received a

These are officers of the famous Irish Brigade. In their assaults against the stone wall, 41 per cent of their almost 1,200 men were lost. They wore sprigs of boxwood in their kepis (since they lacked shamrocks) to designate themselves as the Irish Brigade during the attack.

severe front and enfilade fire, was thrown into partial confusion, and was obliged to fall back under the cover afforded by a depression of ground and the bed of an old canal. From this position they were withdrawn and re-formed behind the railroad, and finally stationed for the night in a position in front of the slaughter house, parallel to Caroline Street.

'The 2nd Brigade advanced in good order ... [but] ... they were exposed to a heavy fire. The picket line was held by the One hundred and third New York Volunteers'. Getty's damage was less severe than other Union divisions – one officer killed, seven commissioned officers wounded; 12 enlisted men killed; 200 enlisted men wounded; 64 enlisted men missing. 'Total, 284'.

At the end of the day, Lee still held Marye's Heights. Burnside held Fredericksburg under Confederate guns, and a large portion of his troops had been mauled. He was appalled at the carnage, and felt it was his fault. He must have glared at the heights and gritted his teeth, resolving that tomorrow he would take them even if he had to lead the charge himself!

Taken after Fredericksburg, at a Confederate prison in Charleston, South Carolina, the soldiers shown were members of the 69th New York who had been captured. Their stances and direct stares are hardly those of defeated prisoners.

This shot of the Marye House on Marye's Heights shows surprisingly little damage (note chips in the columns) after the six Union assaults. Most of the fighting was at the stone wall below and slightly to right of the front of the house

FRANKLIN'S FRONT

Burnside wanted a co-ordinated offensive, but the initiative rapidly escaped him. Meade's attack on Jackson's position became the one bright spot and would become the source of many 'what-might-have-beens' afterward, for Meade had a fleeting success where others had none.

The late afternoon of 12 December Burnside met with Franklin, Smith, and Reynolds to discuss the thrust of the following day. Franklin was to break through Jackson's line to seize the military road and roll up the Confederate flank.

Franklin's orders read: 'General Hardie will carry this dispatch to you and remain with you during the day... Keep your whole command in position for a rapid movement down the Old Richmond Road, and... send out at once a division at least... to pass below Smithfield, to seize, if *possible* [italics mine], the height near Captain Hamilton's, on this side of the Massaponax.

A naturally cautious commander, Franklin studied Burnside's admonition to keep his line of retreat open and to take care when moving in fog. Perhaps he interpreted this to mean that he was not to move until the fog lifted or visibility greatly improved. Regardless, to Franklin the orders seemed conditional and clear.

Soldiers in Franklin's theatre clumped near bridge-heads, for all knew that if they were cut off from those tenuous lifelines, Stuart's cavalry would be upon them like merciless wolves. Franklin was only too aware of the delicate situation in town and at Stafford Heights. He moved slowly, watching for the least Southern reaction.

Burnside ordered Sumner's men massed in town or at the Upper and Middle Crossings, kept much of Hooker's command in reserve, and sent Franklin south of town to give Lee, Jackson, and Stuart something to think about.

Franklin might break Jackson's line, and could possibly sweep north and roll the Confederate flank, but unless he pressed the Southerners sharply, Burnside feared they would swarm across the RF&P railroad track and force his Grand Divisions back to the water's edge. As ordered, Franklin displayed his men, moving them south from town in a line that stretched to Hamilton's Crossing, but he kept more than sufficient reserves to protect the bridges, his line of retreat.

Securing and guarding the bridgehead appeared foremost in his mind when he ordered the advance. Reynolds, Smith, and Bayard's men were already west of the river. In his report, Franklin described troop disposition and the terrain, calling the ground 'generally a plain... cultivated and much cut up by hedges and ditches. The Old Richmond Road traverses the plain... about 1 mile from the river and nearly parallel to it... bordered on both sides by an earthen parapet and ditch, and is an

exceedingly strong feature in the defense of the ground, had the enemy chosen to hold it. On the right of my position is Deep Run, and on the left, about 1 mile in front of Reynolds, is Massaponax Creek... [both] tributaries of the Rappahannock. The plain is bordered by a range of high hills in front... from Fredericksburg to the Massaponax, nearly parallel to the river. In front of and nearly parallel to the Old Richmond Road, and about 500 or 600 yards from it, at the foot of the range of hills, is the railroad. The ravine through which Deep Creek runs passes through the hills near the center of my front. Two brigades of... Smith's corps were in front of Deep Creek, forming the extreme right. The remainder [were positioned] in rear... to the left of Deep Creek, Reynolds' Corps being about 1 mile from the Massaponax. The enemy had artillery on the hills and in the valley of Deep Creek, in the wood to Reynolds right, and on the Massaponax so that the whole field was surrounded by it except the right flank. His [Stonewall Jackson's] infantry appeared in all directions around the position. In front of Reynolds'

Major John Pelham moved a battery of two guns and some rifles as skirmishers in front of the Confederate lines. For over an hour they harassed Meade's advance, limbering and moving the guns every time that they were located by the Union artillery.

right the forest extends to the Old Richmond Road, coming nearer the river there than at any other point in the vicinity of my position. The railroad traverses the forest'.

At 0830 hours, Franklin began to move his men into attack formation. Major General George Meade's 3rd Division, I Corps, formed an attack column between 0900 and 1000 hours and thrust forward and then shifted down toward Massaponax, supported by Gibbon (2nd Division, I Corps) to his right and Doubleday (1st Division, I Corps) to his left.

Franklin informed Burnside at 0900 hours: 'General Meade just moved out. Doubleday supports him. Meade's skirmishers engaged, however, at once with the enemy's skirmishers. Battery opening, on Meade probably, from position on Old Richmond Road'.

When Meade moved away from the river and started toward the railroad cut and Hamilton's Crossing, Confederate skirmishers were on top of him. Both Jackson's batteries ahead and Stuart's batteries to his left opened fire from the Confederate lines.

Having received permission from Stuart, Major John Pelham moved a battery of two guns and some dismounted rifles as skirmishers forward of the Southern lines. When Meade moved forward, they opened fire. Throughout the next hour Pelham harassed Meade's attempts to advance near Hamilton's Crossing by firing, limbering, and moving when Union artillery got his range, and then unlimbering and firing again. Even after one of his guns was out of commission, Pelham continued to annoy Meade's Pennsylvanians with the remaining one.

Pelham started the ball by firing his 12-pounder when the Federals were 400 yards away. The sudden and unexpected attack took Meade's line from the flank, the shot passing down the line. As one of Pelham's gunners, Pvt. G. W. Shreve later stated, 'We could hear... a medley of voices, but could not see them... only a few hundred yards distant. The fog commenced to lift... and exposed... a grand spectacle of marshaled soldiery... in our immediate front'. When Pelham's battery fired on Meade's left, Shreve said, 'The unexpected presence of our guns so close... seemed to paralyze them, and throw them into disorder. Instead of rushing... us... they were evidently afraid of us... judging... that we had a strong force concealed behind the hedge. The rain of shot and shell upon us was terrific ... [but] ... The enemy's gunners shot too high and so we escaped'. Pelham moved the gun and his skirmishers.

A Union soldier, Corporal B. Alexander, reminisced, 'A cannon boomed out... at close range, seemingly on the Bowling Green Road. The order was given, 'Down'. This single gun... soon got the range... on the flanks of some of our regiments'.

Now other Confederate artillery fell silent as visibility improved so they could see Stafford Heights, lest they reveal their positions to the watchful Union gunners there. Frustrated Union artillery commanders sent shells blindly onto the slopes where the concealed Confederates waited beneath the canopy of partially denuded winter trees.

At 1100 hours Franklin dictated the following message to Burnside: 'Meade advanced half a mile, and holds on. Infantry of enemy in woods in front of extreme left, also in front of Howe. No loss so far of great

This is the site of Sumner's crossings. Nearly a mile down river Major General Franklin's men created three pontoon bridges (one of which was suitable only for infantry) and crossed to assault the Confederate line, 13 December 1862.

importance, General Vinton badly but not dangerously wounded'. He finished with: 'Later – Reynolds has been forced to develop his whole line. An attack of some force of enemy's troops on our left seems probable, as far as can now be judged. Stoneman has been directed to cross one division to support our left. Report of cavalry pickets from the other side of the river, that enemy's troops were moving down the river on this side during the latter part of the night. Howe's pickets have reported movements in their front, same direction. Still they have a strong force well posted, with batteries there'.

The Confederate troops spotted earlier moving along the western bank were probably Stuart's and D. H. Hill's men closing up from Guinea Station. Confederate artillery also moved into position near here, although the Union report appears to refer to infantry.

About noon Meade and Gibbon started moving their divisions toward a few houses in a small concave formed by the adjacent hillsides. At 800 yards, Confederate guns thundered, sundering the advancing Union infantry. Federal gun captains sighted the Southern muzzle flashes and conducted counter-battery fire for an hour, their greater numbers slowly forcing Jackson's guns to fall silent or be destroyed.

By 1300 hours Meade's troops had overrun the railroad embankment and were scrabbling on the lower slopes of the hills toward Gregg, who was supported on his right by Archer and on his left by Lane. When the Confederate artillery fire lessened, Meade's men pushed forward, despite constant fire from Pelham's guns, which kept moving, and charged the Southern line at the edge of the woods south of Bernard's cabins, hitting an area held by Lane, Gregg, and Archer. Gibbon, who had started with Meade, was entangled in fighting for the railroad embankment and was soon left behind as the Pennsylvanians moved forward relentlessly. Reynolds called artillery fire in front of Meade's advance to help him overcome Southern troops who laid down heavy rifle fire.

Major General William Buel Franklin read Burnside's orders and fixated on their conditional terms; he was more concerned about protecting his lines of retreat than following orders and knocking a hole in Jackson's line to roll up the Confederate right flank.

At 1315 hours Franklin sent Burnside the following message: 'Heavy engagements of infantry. Enemy in force where battery is. Meade is assaulting the hill; will report in a few minutes again'.

At 1325 hours Franklin updated the commander, saying: 'Meade is in the woods in his front, seems to be able to hold on. Reynolds will push Gibbon in, if necessary. The battery and woods referred to must be near Hamilton's house. The infantry firing is prolonged and quite heavy. Things look well enough. Men in fine spirits'.

About 1330 hours Confederate General 'Stonewall' Jackson realized the strength of the Union threat. He ordered Taliaferro into the woods, intent on dislodging Meade and possibly shattering the Union flank.

Gibbon's division was to have been in line behind Meade's as reinforcements and reserves. He moved his men forward to support the attack so Confederates wouldn't isolate Meade. When Pelham's battery was ordered to vacate the spot above Hamilton's Crossing and return to Confederate lines, Doubleday's 1st Division advanced, took the crossroads, and positioned units facing south and west to discourage further

MEADE'S BRIEF BREAKTHROUGH AT HAMILTON'S CROSSING

1300–1400 HOURS SATURDAY, 13 DECEMBER 1862

Gibbon has been in line behind Meade's command as reinforcements and reserves. He moves his men forward to support the attack and reinforce his rear so the Confederates can't isolate Meade. When Pelham's battery is ordered to vacate the spot above Hamilton's Crossing and return to Confederate lines, Doubleday's men take the crossroads and face units south and west to discourage further Confederate attacks. Newton begins moving south but not east while Smith guards the bridgehead. Birney stays at the stage road.

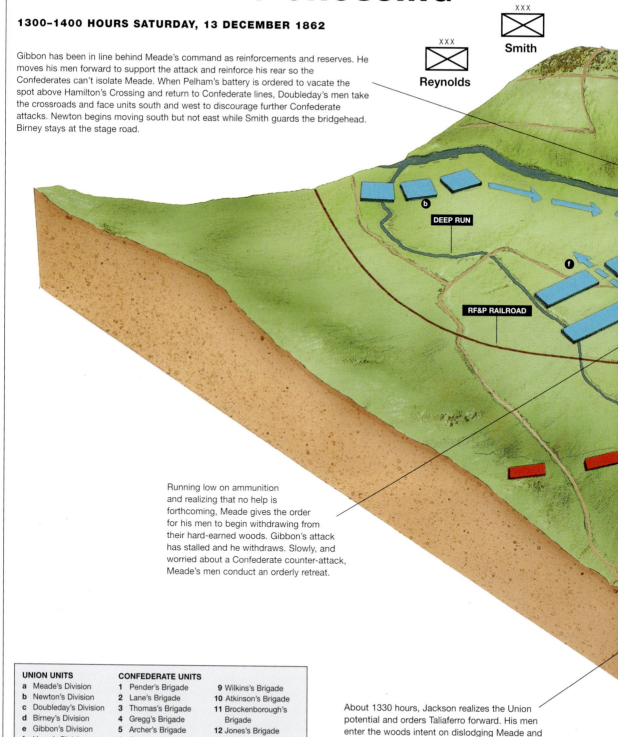

XXX
Smith

XXX
Reynolds

DEEP RUN

RF&P RAILROAD

Running low on ammunition and realizing that no help is forthcoming, Meade gives the order for his men to begin withdrawing from their hard-earned woods. Gibbon's attack has stalled and he withdraws. Slowly, and worried about a Confederate counter-attack, Meade's men conduct an orderly retreat.

UNION UNITS	CONFEDERATE UNITS	
a Meade's Division	**1** Pender's Brigade	**9** Wilkins's Brigade
b Newton's Division	**2** Lane's Brigade	**10** Atkinson's Brigade
c Doubleday's Division	**3** Thomas's Brigade	**11** Brockenborough's Brigade
d Birney's Division	**4** Gregg's Brigade	**12** Jones's Brigade
e Gibbon's Division	**5** Archer's Brigade	**13** Warren's Brigade
f Howe's Division	**6** Stuart's Division	**14** Hoke's Brigade
	7 Pendleton's Brigade	**15** D. H. Hill's Division
	8 Paxton's Brigade	

About 1330 hours, Jackson realizes the Union potential and orders Taliaferro forward. His men enter the woods intent on dislodging Meade and possibly sundering the Union flank.

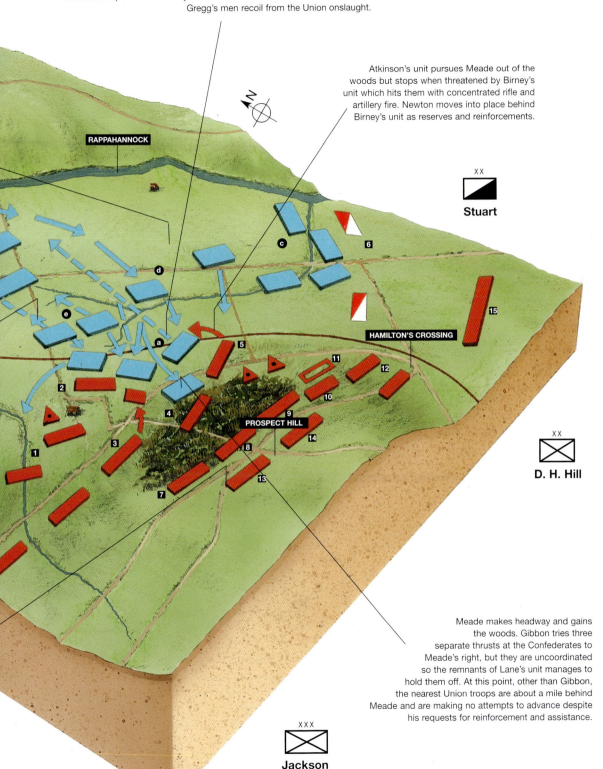

After nearly a sixty minute artillery duel, Meade pushes forward, despite constant fire from Pelham's guns which keep moving. His men charge the Southern line at the edge of the woods and south of Bernard's cabins, hitting an area held by Lane, Gregg, and Archer. Lane's right flank crumbles and Meade's troops force their way forward. Archer's command is shattered and Gregg's men recoil from the Union onslaught.

Atkinson's unit pursues Meade out of the woods but stops when threatened by Birney's unit which hits them with concentrated rifle and artillery fire. Newton moves into place behind Birney's unit as reserves and reinforcements.

Meade makes headway and gains the woods. Gibbon tries three separate thrusts at the Confederates to Meade's right, but they are uncoordinated so the remnants of Lane's unit manages to hold them off. At this point, other than Gibbon, the nearest Union troops are about a mile behind Meade and are making no attempts to advance despite his requests for reinforcement and assistance.

RAPPAHANNOCK

HAMILTON'S CROSSING

PROSPECT HILL

X X
Stuart

X X
D. H. Hill

X X X
Jackson

Confederate attacks. Brigadier General John Newton began moving 3rd Division, VI Corps, south but not east, while Major General William F. Smith's VI Corps guarded the bridgehead. Brigadier General David Birney (1st Division, III Corps, Center Grand Division, on loan from Hooker) remained at the stage road, watchful for a counterattack.

In his report Meade noted that the slope 'to the railroad from the extreme left of the space of 300 or 400 yards was clear; beyond this it was wooded, the woods extending across the hollow and in front of the railroad. The plateau on our side was level and cultivated ground up to the crest of the hollow, where there was quite a fall to the railroad. The enemy occupied the wooded heights, the line of railroad, and the wood in front. Owing to the wood, nothing could be seen of them, while all our movements on the cleared ground were exposed to their view.'

Meade's men were aligned thus: '1st Brigade in line of battle on the crest of the hollow, and facing the railroad, with the Sixth Regiment deployed as skirmishers; the 2nd Brigade in rear of the 1st 300 paces; the 3rd Brigade by the flank, its right flank being a few rods to the rear of the 1st Brigade, having the Ninth Regiment deployed on its flank as skirmishers and flankers, and the batteries between the 1st and 2nd Brigades. This disposition had scarcely been made when the enemy opened a brisk fire from a battery posted on the Bowling Green Road, the shot from which took the command from the left and rear'.

To protect his left rear, Meade ordered 3rd Brigade to face left. Between it and the 1st Brigade, his men formed two sides of a square (an 'L') and Cpt. Dunbar Ransom's (B/5th US) and Cpt. James Cooper's (B/1st Pennsylvania Light) batteries moved to a knoll on their left to open fire on the Southerners, aided by some of Doubleday's batteries. Union General Ferger Jackson deployed two companies as skirmishers, who drove the Confederates back. Attacks from their left and rear ceased, so Meade continued his advance.

At 1340 hours Franklin sent Burnside an update: 'Meade having carried a portion of the enemy's position in the woods, we have 300 prisoners, enemy's battery on extreme left retired. Tough work; men fight well. Gibbon has advanced to Meade's right, men fight well, driving the enemy. Meade has suffered severely. Doubleday to Meade's left not engaged'.

Luck was with Meade when he hit the Confederate line, making Lane's right flank crumble and his men forced their way forward. Archer's command was shattered and Gregg's men recoiled from the heavy Union onslaught. Earlier A. P. Hill had studied the wooded and boggy area which was nearly 600 yards wide and thought it impassable, putting his troops elsewhere and leaving it open. This inward salient let Meade's men reach wooded cover, move uphill, and fall upon Brigadier General Maxcy Gregg's line west of the military road.

Meade's soldiers plunged through the woods onto the surprised South Carolinians. Successive waves of Union soldiers expanded the gap both left and right, opening a hole in the Confederate defensive position, hitting the flanks of Archer's and Lane's units, forcing them back and widening the gap still further.

Meade later stated, 'The 1st Brigade... advanced several hundred

Major General William F. Smith led VI Corps at Fredericksburg. His corps was largely concerned with holding the Union line and keeping lines of retreat across the pontoon bridges open. Had Franklin sent his corps forward aggressively, Meade might have succeeded.

yards over cleared ground, driving the enemy's skirmishers before them, till they reached the woods... in front of the railroad, which they entered, driving the enemy out of them to the... temporary defenses [west of the railroad]... The brigade... drove them... up the heights in their front, though owing to a heavy fire being received on their right flank, they obliqued to that side, but continued forcing the enemy back till they had crossed the crest of the hill, crossed a main road which runs along the crest, and reached open ground on the other side, where they were assailed by a severe fire from a large force in their front, and, at the same time, the enemy opened a battery which completely enfiladed them from the right flank'.

Gregg's men felt secure on the hilltop west of the road, and were unprepared for the sudden Union onslaught. Their arms were stacked, and they were chatting or eating when broken Confederate troops pursued by Union troops erupted from woods supposedly impassable. Some men sprang into action and fired at the advancing shapes, while others grabbed their weapons in confusion.

General Gregg thought the advancing Union soldiers must have been Confederates and rode down the line telling his men to hold their fire until they were sure of their targets – and sure their targets were not other Southerners. Still, some fired into the advancing mass. One of Gregg's brigade sergeants later laconically commented, 'Hope they're not our men, for I've killed one'. Because of Gregg's efforts, Southern fire diminished, and stopped. This was their undoing, for broken soldiers poured through their lines and suddenly the Union soldiers were upon them.

While they approached, Gregg held fire, unwilling to shoot fellow Southerners, feeling they were falling back to re-form in safety. He rode up and down the line, ordering his men to be steady and refrain from firing. Sharp-eyed Union soldiers saw the general from South Carolina and fired, knocking Maxcy Gregg from his horse; he was mortally wounded. With Gregg down, the South Carolinians sagged and threatened to collapse before the Union charge, but although confused and leaderless, they did not break.

Colonel Hoke, positioned behind Gregg, ordered his men to ready themselves, and then ordered them forward to bolster the stunned South Carolinians. The Union troops sensed victory and cheered as they advanced, and then they ran headlong into Hoke's men, who met them with lead and bayonets. Hoke's men let out an eerie rebel yell and rushed toward the advancing Pennsylvanians. One Union officer said, ' I have never, since I was born, heard so fearful a noise as a rebel yell. It is nothing like a hurrah, but rather a regular wildcat screech'. The Pennsylvanians broke and started back down hill toward the railroad cut, attempting to re-form, but were hard-pressed by the Confederates.

Confederate reserves under Taliaferro and Early charged through the woods, crashing into Meade's Pennsylvanians, halting the Union advance. Fierce hand-to-hand fighting ensued, while Union troops

Franklin had little success overall. Meade's Pennsylvanians forced a hole in Southern defenses and fought up a hill to fall upon Maxcy Gregg's unsuspecting South Carolinians. Meade was bitter that his breakthrough was unsupported and his men had to fall back.

awaited reinforcements and Southerners tried to plug the gap. While the Union advance stalled, Lane and Archer rallied their disorganized brigades into new lines at the sides of the Union path of advance. It was over, but Meade's men did not know it yet and were unwilling to give up ground they had fought so hard to gain.

Meade later recalled, 'Second Brigade, which advanced in rear of the First, after reaching the railroad, was assailed with so severe a fire on their right flank that the Fourth regiment halted and formed, faced to the right, to repel this attack. The other regiments... inclined in that direction and ascended the heights, the Third going up as the One hundred and twenty-first of the brigade was retiring. The Third continued to advance, and reached nearly the same point as the 1st Brigade, but was compelled to withdraw for the same reason'. Fighting was chaotic, from tree to tree, deadfall to deadfall in the woods. 'The 3rd Brigade had not advanced over 100 yards when the battery on the height to its left was remanned, and poured a destructive fire into its ranks.

'The enemy was driven from the railroad, his rifle pits, and breastworks for over half a mile. Over 200 prisoners taken and several standards, when the advancing line encountered the heavy reinforcements of the enemy, who, recovering from the effects of our assault... poured in such a destructive fire from all three directions as to compel the line to fall back'.

Meade looked for support, but Gibbon was nowhere to be found. His men were tired and in advance of Union lines. Ammunition was running low. Still, he had a breakthrough if only reinforcements could get there. He sent to Franklin, urgently requesting support from some of the 20,000 men in reserve. Franklin sent no support.

Taliaferro's men hit the weakened Pennsylvanians with everything they had. Artillery, buck and ball, and bayonet made Meade's men, who were starting to run low on ammunition, grudgingly give ground. Step by step, glade by glade, Confederates shoved the Federal soldiers out of the woods.

Telegraph Road was the key to the Southern positions along the series of hills going south from Fredericksburg. Burnside hoped Franklin could fight through to it and move north, to join with Sumner at Fredericksburg and force the Confederates off the crests of the hills.

Burnside received the following message from Franklin about the happenings at 1415 hours: 'Gibbon and Meade driven back from the woods. Newton gone forward. Jackson's corps of the enemy attacks on the left. General Gibbon slightly wounded. General Bayard mortally wounded by a shell. Things do not look as well on Reynolds' front, still we'll have new troops in soon'.

Meade was worried that he'd be overrun. 'Perceiving the danger of the too great penetration of my line, without support, I dispatched several staff officers both to General Gibbon's command and General Birney's... urging... support. A brigade of Birney's advanced to our relief just as my men were withdrawn from the wood, and Gibbon's division advanced into the wood on our right in time to assist materially in the safe withdrawal of my broken line'. Low on ammunition and realizing no help was forthcoming, Meade gave the order to begin withdrawing from their hard-earned woods. Gibbon's attack stalled and he withdrew. Slowly, and worried about a Confederate counter-attack, Meade's men conducted an orderly retreat while he fumed that he had not been given support.

At 1425 hours Franklin replied to an inquiry from Burnside: 'Dispatch received. Franklin will do his best. New troops gone in, will report soon again'.

Gibbon tried three separate thrusts at the Confederates to Meade's right, but they were uncoordinated so the remnants of Lane's unit managed to fight them off. At this point, other than Gibbon, the nearest Union troops were about a mile behind Meade and making no attempt to advance, despite his requests for assistance. Atkinson's Georgians pursued Meade out of the woods, stopping only when threatened by one of Birney's units (114th Pennsylvania, Collis' Zouaves) which hit them with concentrated rifle and artillery fire at the railroad grade. There the Georgians stopped and slowly, reluctantly, withdrew. Newton moved into place behind Birney's unit as reserves and reinforcements.

At 1500 Burnside got a message from Franklin: 'Reynolds seems to be holding his own. Things look better somewhat'. It was followed at 1540 hours by a less optimistic message: 'Gibbon and Meade's divisions are badly used up, and I fear another advance on the enemy on our left cannot be made this afternoon. Doubleday's Division will replace Meade's as soon as it can be collected, and if it be done in time, of course another attack will be made. The enemy are in force in the woods on our left towards Hamilton's, and are threatening the safety of that portion of our line. They seem to have detached a portion of their force to our front where Howe and Brooks are now engaged. Brooks has some prisoners, and is down to the railroad. Just as soon as the left is safe, our forces here will be prepared for a front attack, but it may be too late this afternoon. Indeed, we are engaged in front anyhow. Not withstanding the unpleasant items I relate, the morale generally of the troops is good'.

Meade recounted: 'An unsuccessful attempt was made to re-form the division in the hollow in front of the batteries. Failing in this, the command was re-formed beyond the Bowling Green Road and marched to the ground occupied the night before, where it was held in reserve till the night of the 15th, when we recrossed the river'.

The final round in Franklin's salvo of messages told Burnside at 1630 hours: 'The enemy is still to our left and front. An attack on our batteries in front has been repulsed. A new attack has just opened on our left, but the left is safe, though it is too late to advance either to the left or front'. The fierce give and take on Franklin's front was winding down as daylight ebbed.

Meade ends his report by attaching the butcher's bill – '179 killed, 1,082 wounded, and 509 missing... this large loss being 40 percent'. He concluded that although he regretted not being able to take and hold the enemy position, without reinforcements, holding the ground gained was impossible and that he had no desire to needlessly sacrifice his troops. He felt that 'the best troops would be justified in withdrawing without loss of honor'. Meade felt he could have held the ground gained if he had been supported. Four months later, at Chancellorsville, this may have come out when Hooker stopped the victorious Union troops from advancing and ordered them to resume their earlier positions. Meade snapped, 'If he can't hold the top of the hill, how does he expect to hold the bottom of it?'

Stonewall Jackson was galled at the Union flight and resurgence. It appeared they were beaten. They had created a salient and rushed into the heart of Confederate defenses where they had almost been decimated, but now they retreated to the safety of the RP&F grade. Hoping to goad them into another charge, he ordered the Rockbridge artillery to open fire. Instead of provoking a charge to silence these guns, or forcing the Union to withdraw even further, the Rockbridge battery's fire prompted Union gunners to counter-battery fire. In the ensuing storm of shell, Colonel Coleman, who was trying to get the battery to stop firing, was hit and killed. The order to cease fire was repeated and Confederate gunners dived for any cover they could find while gouts of earth blew upwards from the Union shells.

Franklin positioned his men around the bridge and on the plain. They wouldn't advance, but they wouldn't yield their position either, and as night fell, Confederates on the mountain and Federals on the plain watched one another's positions, looking for any sign of movement that might indicate a charge or renewed attack.

When he received word of Franklin's weak thrust, Burnside saw Jackson's advance as a sign that the Confederate position on Marye's Heights has weakened and that his 'diversion' was working. He ordered French to begin the first attack on the stone wall. The Right Grand Division of the Army of the Potomac began its ordeal under fire.

This pontoon bridge is similar to the ones south of Fredericksburg used by Franklin's Grand Division. Unlike the Upper and Middle bridges, which were heavily contested, the Lower Crossing went up almost without resistance.

CLOSING MOVES

J. E. B. Stuart's cavalry was at Guiney Station and moved north to block off Northern advances down the RF&P or the Old Richmond Stage Road when Franklin's men crossed to the west side of the Rappahannock.

At the close of day, 13 December 1862, it was apparent to all that Burnside's plan had been disastrous; moreover, the specter of the missed opportunity on Franklin's front hung heavy in the air. Burnside was not imaginative, but he was honest: he had failed.

Burnside gathered his commanders to decide what to do next. No one knows what ran through his mind, but when he proposed one final assault against Marye's Heights, led by himself, silence fell over his commanders. Officers looked on, stunned. Such an attempt was suicide, they thought.

Psychologically, Burnside may have felt like Romans of old given the caveat of 'come home victorious or on your shield'. He had not wanted command. He had told the powers in Washington that others were better suited than he. Burnside had known his shortcomings – and Fredericksburg had proven him right. Perhaps he felt his presence leading the charge could make the difference, or perhaps he wanted to atone, to die. Regardless, he announced he would lead the assault of IX Corps at dawn on 14 December. Hearing Burnside's almost suicidal plan, his top commanders protested that he could not lead an attack, and that no one else should either, for had not six attempts shown how well defended was Marye's Heights? Gradually Burnside let them talk him out of it, relenting. There would be no attack. This campaign for Fredericksburg was over. After Burnside announced his intentions, his commanders breathed a collective sigh of relief.

Although stories of heroism in battle, such as the saving of the Irish Brigade's colors, abound, there is another kind of heroism, one where humanity precedes military precedence and a man risks his life trying to help his enemies. Such a soldier was Sergeant Richard Kirkland of the 2nd South Carolina.

After the battle, the wounded were in terrible torment. Some groaned in pain, others cried for their mothers or sweethearts, some begged in raspy voices for water while a few, in their pain, begged to be killed. In front of the stone wall, bodies of living and wounded entwined. Soldiers of both sides watched the no man's land between, potshotting any individual movement that seemed to signal an offensive. To make matters worse, the night of 13 December was brutally cold. The litany of moaning carried to both lines, and some men put their hands over their ears to try and quell the sounds of pain.

At General Joseph Kershaw's position near Marye's Heights, the

wounded beyond the stone wall lay in agony, their voices a grating drone. Most were Yankees, but a few were Confederates. After the bloodbath of the day, Union pickets watched for Southern scavengers and fired if they saw someone sneaking from Southern lines near the wounded. Likewise, Southern sharpshooters were watchful in case Burnside attacked again.

On 14 December, a Sunday, Union stretcher bearers were busy within their lines. Still, by nightfall many wounded in no man's land were untended, their moans and crying making men of both sides edgy as they watched the far ranks for signs of aggressive movement. Lee expected Burnside to attack again, and if not in the same place, at least to probe elsewhere, but no attack occurred.

In later years, General Kershaw related that he was sitting in the Stevens house when Sergeant Kirkland approached him and asked if the general could hear the pleas of the wounded, adding, 'I can't stand this'.

Kershaw listened as Kirkland continued, 'All night and day I have heard those poor people crying for water, and I can stand it no longer. I... ask permission... to give them water'.

Kershaw studied the slim Sergeant with the well groomed mustache and carefully mended uniform. 'You could get a bullet through your head the moment you stepped over the wall'.

'I know that; but if you'll let me, I'm willing to try it'.

Kershaw paused and then consented, saying, 'The sentiment which actuates you is so noble that I will not refuse your request, trusting that God may protect you'. Then Kershaw added that Kirkland was not allowed to use a white flag, however, as that might lead the Union troops to think that Kershaw's men were surrendering.

Permission granted, Kirkland ran outside. He gathered canteens from his messmates, made certain they were full, and then slung them over his shoulders and vaulted the wall. When surprised Union pickets saw him, at first they aimed, thinking him a scavenger, and then they noticed he carried canteens and was heading for the nearest wounded man, a wounded Union soldier. Kneeling beside the pleading man, Kirkland raised the wounded man's head and put the canteen to his parched lips while the soldier gulped the water to ease his fever-ridden body. Finished he placed a knapsack under the injured man's head and proceeded to the next wounded man while soldiers of both sides watched in amazement. For some, he straightened wounded or broken limbs, and placed their overcoats on them like blankets, leaving a full canteen and taking their empty one as he moved on to the next man. The nature of his mission gradually dawned on both sides as he made the rounds to help Union and Confederate alike, and soldiers eased down rifle hammers to watch him move from one huddled form to the next. He ministered every man in his part of the field for over an hour and a half, giving water, covering them, and easing their suffering as best he could. He returned to the stone wall, and later men began referring to him as 'the Angel of Marye's Heights'. Kirkland died two years later in the fighting at Chickamauga. Kershaw said of him, 'He has bequeathed to the world an example which dignifies our common humanity'.

On 15 December a truce was finally arranged and both Confederate and Union stretcher bearers removed the wounded from the field with impunity. That night a freezing, driving rain soaked the town, as if the heavens were weeping for the waste of life. Laying dirt and straw on the

Sergeant Richard Kirkland earned his sobriquet of 'The Angel of Marye's Heights' by going out into the no mans land between the Confederate and Union lines on the morning of 14 December to minister to the wounded who had been stranded there for a day and a night.

pontoon bridges to muffle the sound of their passage, the Army of the Potomac withdrew. The next morning, Confederate pickets were astounded to see that where a great army had encamped, there was nothing.

Southern newspapers were elated. Northern papers heard of the disaster and wanted blood. Yes, Burnside and his generals were cursed, but Lincoln bore the brunt of the Northern ill-will. One senator's comment was vitriolic, claiming, Lincoln was incompetent and 'those fool or traitor generals are wasting time and yet more precious blood in indecisive battles and delays'.

Burnside reported to Halleck that the loss of the battle was based on the tardy arrival of the pontoon bridges, but he bore full responsibility for the debacle because he had insisted on forcing an engagement at Fredericksburg. Lincoln read the report and then showed great compassion in his response to the men of the Army of the Potomac, when he stated, 'Although you were not successful, the attempt was not an error, nor the failure other than an accident. The courage... you... maintained... against an entrenched foe, and the consummate skill and success with which you crossed and recrossed the river in the face of the enemy, show that you possess all the qualities of a great army'. Lincoln had faith in the men, if not in their leaders.

Hood held part of the ridge line near where Gregg's men were positioned. This is the only known picture of Hood's Texans in uniform. Note the long frock coats and mixture of headgear. The photo was shot near the action at Seven Pines.

At Fredericksburg this Union battery was in position on Stafford Heights, overlooking the town and the plains below. They could protect Meade's advance, but once he closed with Gregg, they were helpless for fear of hitting Federal troops with friendly fire.

THE MUD MARCH

Burnside planned to take the battle south again. There was a stain on his name and he was determined to erase it. Fredericksburg had become a symbol of personal failure to him. Despite the fact that many units were in winter quarters, he felt this was a good time to continue a Union offensive, if for no other reason than to surprise the Southerners. He planned to move the army across the northern fords above Fredericksburg, despite the inclement weather, and to move on Richmond.

Major John Pelham, with Stuart's permission, moved two artillery pieces in front of Southern lines to harass Meade's advancing soldiers. One piece was destroyed, but he continued to fire, move, and harass the Federal soldiers with the remaining one until ordered back to the line.

On 30 December his cavalry started to move, leading the advance. The weather worsened. Rain and sleet pounded the snowy ground, turning roads into morasses of putty-like mud which clung to wagon wheels, hooves, stiffened pants, and triple weighted soldiers' brogans. Icy rain trickled down the men's necks as they massed and moved toward the crossing point Burnside had designated. Movement was labored, for not only was the weather poor, their hearts were not in it.

When Burnside announced his plans, the commanders of his three Grand Divisions met. This was lunacy. Burnside would get them all killed! General Hooker railed at Sumner and Franklin, trying to get them to act. Two generals, Newton and Brooks, were encouraged to take their destinies in their own hands and visit Washington to speak with Lincoln. Once there, they voiced their fears that the campaign would end as badly as Fredericksburg and that many lives would be thrown away in the process. Lincoln listened and then let them return to their commands.

Burnside planned to move the Army of the Potomac upriver and cross, circling southward to entrap Lee. Ironically, he planned to meet Lee at Fredericksburg again, as if by meeting and besting his foe on the same ground they had met on earlier he could erase his failure. He set the army in motion, intending to cross the river around New Year's Day. When Lincoln heard of Burnside's suggested plan of action, he sent a telegram, commanding, 'I have good reason for saying you must not make a general movement of the army without letting me know'.

Burnside stopped, and turned his army around. When he learned of his officers visiting Lincoln, he was furious and tendered his resignation, to which Lincoln replied 'I deplore the lack of concurrence between you and your general officers, but I do not see the remedy. I do not see yet how I could profit by changing the command of the Army of the Potomac, and if I did, I should not wish to do it by accepting the resignation of your commission'.

However, Lincoln had stopped the Mud March and had told Burnside return to winter quarters. The men had been miserable marching out and were just as miserable returning. Morale, which was never high, plummeted.

Burnside requested that Hooker be relieved of command in General Order 8, which he forwarded to Lincoln for his approval. It read:

General Order 8	**Hdqrs. Army of the Potomac**
	23 January 1863

I. General Joseph Hooker, Major General of volunteers and Brigadier General US army, having been guilty of unjust and unnecessary criticisms of the actions of his superior officers, and of the authorities, and having, by the general tone of his conversation, endeavored to create distrust in the minds of officers who have associated with him, and having, by omissions and otherwise made reports and statements which were calculated to create incorrect impressions, and for habitually speaking in disparaging terms of other officers, is hereby dismissed the service of the United States as a man unfit to hold an important commission during a crisis like the present, when so much patience, charity, confidence, consideration, and patriotism are due from every soldier in the field. This order is issued subject to the approval of the President of the United States.

II. Brigadier General W. T. H. Brooks commanding the 1st Division, Sixth Army Corps , for complaining of the policy of the government, and for using language tending to demoralize his command, is, subject to the approval of the President, dismissed from the military service of the United States.

III. Brigadier General John Newton, commanding 3rd Division, Sixth Army Corps, and Brig. Gen. John Cochrane, commanding 1st Brigade, 3rd Division, Sixth Army Corps, for going to the President of the United States with criticisms upon the plans of their command-

Lieutenant General Ambrose P. Hill held the lower angle of the Southern line. He thought the ground in front of Gregg impassable, so it was only lightly defended. Gregg, Archer, and Lane were brigade commanders of his. Meade broke between Archer and Lane to assault Gregg, who was positioned uphill, to the rear of Lane and Archer.

Months later at Chancellorsville, Federal gunners took almost the same positions to shell Confederates in town, along Telegraph Road, and near Marye's Heights. This photo, taken on 3 May 1863 at Fredericksburg, shows a Union battery in action.

ing officer, are, subject to the approval of the President, dismissed from the military service of the United States.

IV. It being evident that the following named officers can be of no further service to this army, they are hereby relieved from duty and will report, in person, without delays, to the Adjutant-general, US Army: Maj. Gen. W. B. Franklin, commanding Left Grand Division, Maj. Gen. W. F. Smith, commanding Sixth Corps; Brig. Gen. Edward Ferrero, commanding 2nd Brigade, 2nd Division, Ninth Army Corps; Brig. Gen. John Cochrane, commanding 1st Brigade, 3rd Division, Sixth Corps; Lieut. Col. J. H. Taylor. Assistant adjutant-general, Right Grand Division.

By command of Maj. Gen. A. E. Burnside:
Lewis Richmond
Assistant Adjutant

Burnside intended a clean sweep. Of his Grand Division commanders, only loyal Sumner was unnamed. Burnside took the order to Washington, and with it, his resignation. He asked Lincoln to accept one or the other. Lincoln saw no way to salvage Burnside, and so he let him return to the Army of the Potomac, but already he prepared for the next commander.

On 25 January Lincoln responded to Burnside's requests with General Order 20, dated 25 January which read:

General Order 20 **War Department, Adjutant General's Office**
Washington, January 25, 1863

I. The President of the United States has directed:

1. That Maj. Gen. A. E. Burnside, at his own request, be relieved from command of the Army of the Potomac.

2. That Maj. Gen. E.V. Sumner, at his own request be relieved from duty in the Army of the Potomac.

3. That Maj. Gen. W. B. Franklin be relieved from duty in the Army of the Potomac.

4. That Maj. Gen. J. Hooker be assigned to the command of the Army of the Potomac.

II. The officers relieved as above will report in person to the Adjutant General of the Army.

By order of the Secretary of War:
E. D. Townsend
Assistant Adjutant General

After requesting to be relieved of command several times, Burnside had his wish at last: Lincoln had found another man to lead the Army of the Potomac – Joseph Hooker.

ANALYSIS

Burnside's Fredericksburg Campaign was doomed almost from inception. His generals thought they were better suited than he to command and second-guessed his every move. Franklin and Hooker both thought they should run the Army of the Potomac.

Burnside's strategy received only lukewarm approval and he basically was given permission to take Fredericksburg only because he commanded the Army of the Potomac and not because the plan was brilliant. Halleck never supported Burnside, but then he was non-committal to almost everyone. Lincoln had said the attack would succeed if carried out quickly, but the tardy arrival of the pontoon boats thwarted that part of the plan. Timing was everything. Not only were pontoons late, but the prongs of the attack were not co-ordinated, and once this failing became apparent, the attack should have been called off; instead Burnside chose to continue, with Sumner's wing bearing the responsibility for carrying the plan.

Burnside worried about morale, but there were other ways he could have remedied that; few futile charges into the jaws of death have improved a soldier's outlook. Burnside's thinking was akin to the paradox: 'The beatings will continue until morale improves'.

The Union Army's procrastination in getting materiel to Burnside by the agreed date and excellent Confederate intelligence gave Lee time and information upon which to act. He pulled his army together, put them on the high ground, and awaited Burnside's attack.

Burnside surprised Lee by taking the bait and walking into the trap, marching his men up to Marye's Heights.

Franklin was not aggressive enough in that he had left too many men to guard the path of retreat, and he viewed his conditional

James Archer's brigade was to the right of Lane, behind the railroad tracks. Meade's assault moved his men across the railroad tracks and smashed into Archer's men, who folded, moving back and creating an opening.

General James H. Lane held the left of the Confederate line at the railroad tracks. When Meade's men hit, his men were thrown back in disarray as were Archer's. Meade's men then moved uphill to attack Gregg's position.

General George D. Bayard was a promising Union cavalry commander in Franklin's command. During the artillery barrage he was mortally wounded by Southern shrapnel and died, robbing the Union of a badly needed cavalry leader.

General Maxcy Gregg saw Confederate troops advancing, pursued by Union soldiers. He tried to keep his men from firing into fellow Southerners. A Union marksman saw him riding horse along the line, encouraging his men, and fatally wounded him.

orders as permission not to advance en masse. Meade's breakthrough may never have turned the Confederate flank, but without real and substantial support, it was doomed to failure.

When Franklin failed to carry his position, Burnside could have stopped Sumner's succeeding assaults, but he let them progress. In the end, despite his geniality, Burnside had not been exhibiting false humility when he had said that others were better qualified to command the Army of the Potomac. Lincoln should have listened.

When all was said and done, the cost to the Union Army was 124 officers killed, 654 wounded, and 20 missing. Enlisted casualties were 1,160 killed, 8,964 wounded, and 1,749 missing – a total of 12,653 men, about 10 per cent of the Army of the Potomac.

Lee's losses were 458 killed and 3,743 wounded – a total of 4,201 men; Burnside's were about three times greater – coincidentally the same ratio of men he would have needed to have a reasonable chance of success in a direct frontal assault on the Confederate position.

Longstreet considered Fredericksburg one of the South's finest battles because his men had fought from a prepared position.

The lesson is loud and clear: never assault a prepared position without a flanking movement, or at least three times the numbers of the defenders.

Union failure includes the structure of the Grand Division, which had proved unwieldy and was dismantled when Hooker took over command of the Army of the Potomac. Cavalry also could have been used better.

Hooker learned from Fredericksburg and decided that when he struck, his plans would remain secret; if he ran into Confederate resistance, he would regroup. Just how successful his plans would be was to be decided at Chancellorsville, fought on some of this same ground four months later.

GAMING
FREDERICKSBURG

These guidelines for Fredericksburg game scenarios are general and intended for use with any skirmish, tactical, or grand tactical set of rules.

Fredericksburg has three scenarios – none of them is especially pleasant for the Union, with the possible exception of 3. In setting up a scenario, winning or losing is less important than judging one's performance against that of historical figures. The three scenarios are:

1. Laying the pontoons and establishing a bridgehead
2. The assault on Marye's Heights
3. Meade's assault on Gregg's, Lane's, and Archer's units.

Scenario 1: Pontoniers

The question is not if the Union player will cross, but how long it will take him to cross. Each turn represents one half-hour. There are twelve hours in the game day.

The Confederate player has no more than three brigades to defend the town. The Union player will not define the area he intends to cross, until after the Confederate player has secretly written down his troops' positions. The Confederate player must protect all three areas and will need a 'flying reserve' to defend them.

This photo of new Britains 54mm American Civil War soldiers depicts members of the Irish Brigade in greatcoats assaulting the positions at Fredericksburg.

The scenario involves house to house fighting. The Union player has from dawn till dusk on one day to do as well or better than the actual Union assault troops did. He must not only create and secure a bridge-head, but also must clean out resistance. If both Union and Confederate troops are in an area, no artillery fire can be sent into that sector.

The Confederates have one reserve brigade available after 1500 hours, and whenever a unit falls below 50 per cent of its initial strength, it must be removed from town and withdraw to safety (the west of town or another Southern unit).

Confederates withdrawing from town during daylight hours may be shelled by Union artillery. If the Confederate player still holds the town at dusk with at least one unit having more than 50 per cent of its original strength, he wins. If the Union player runs the Confederates out of town or reduces their numbers so no unit has more than 50 per cent of its original strength, the Union player wins.

Scenario 2: Forlorn Hope

This represents the six Union assaults on the stone wall. One Confederate brigade holds the length of wall, and one other is within 12 inches of its rear. Nine Confederate guns are right rear of the Confederate line on a little hill. Union units attack directly from the front.

Union troops assault in waves containing three regiments each. Union players may not use artillery fire against the stone wall if their players are within 24 inches of it; and because of the nature of the stone wall and parapet, only exposed Union artillery pieces may fire against it as fire from across the river would be too dangerously inaccurate. Confederates may have up to 20 artillery batteries (nine on the Heights and 11 enfilading at the Southern player's discretion).

Fifty yards in front of the stone wall is a rail fence which halves movement in that area until the fence is torn down – one move without firing or moving. After the first wave, charges suffer a 20 per cent movement penalty because of Union casualties, which must be avoided. Prior waves roll dice to determine how many survivors exit, how many are useless (disorganized), and how many may elect to assist the next wave. Those rolling 10 per cent or less exit; those rolling a 90 per cent or greater assist in the next attack. Those with die rolls of 11 per cent – 89 per cent remain in place.

Two hundred yards in front of the stone wall is a depression. Union troops in that are safe from rifle but not artillery fire, either head-on or within a 20 degree arc. Enfilading Confederate units may fire at the depression, but all Southern small arms fire is at extreme range.

The Confederate position is treated as fortified and well protected. All Confederate firing is at a +10 per cent effectiveness because of supported positions; all Union firing is at a -10 per cent for the same reason. After the first assault, Confederates are reinforced by a regiment; after the fourth assault, they are reinforced by a second regiment.

Prior to the assault, the Union player may fire artillery on the stone wall to dislodge or disorganize Confederate resistance. After the first turn, the Union player may only use artillery batteries that are integral to a unit.

Each turn is one half-hour. The assault starts at 1200 with a barrage which ends at 1300 hours. Union artillery may fire in each of the two half-hour phases against the wall, but not afterwards. The Union commander may assault each turn from 1300 hours to 1830 hours, with a half-hour between assaults to remove withdrawing Union troops and set up the next wave of assaulting troops.

Union players may either charge with fixed bayonets or half-move and fire at the regular ground movement (not charge) rate. They may not do both in the same turn. Confederate players get the bonus for being behind hard cover.

To win, the Union players must take the wall by 1900 hours. Anything less is a loss for the Union. To win, the Confederate players must keep the Union troops from taking the wall. Confederates seek to inflict a minimum of 20 per cent losses on each Union unit, and anything less is a loss.

Scenario 3: the Woods

This is Meade's assault on Confederate positions. Each turn is one half-hour. Play starts at 1100 hours and ends at 1800 hours. A Union artillery barrage may last for two turns (each a half-hour) at the start of the game. Confederate artillery casualties are removed immediately.

Each hour starting the turn after Meade contacts Archer's or Lane's unit, Gregg rolls one ten-sided die. The first hour, a 10 per cent or less is needed for him to form; the second, 20 per cent or less; the third, 30 per cent or less; and so forth. Once Gregg makes his die roll, his men realize that Union troops are moving uphill, and they may form, by bringing two units together on the first turn thereafter, and an additional one on every successive hourly turn. But if they do not make the die roll, they do not realize the Union is coming until Meade's men are upon them, and the Union takes them unprepared. Once attacked, they may form at will if they are able.

The scene is a U-shaped hill with a moderate slope. The bottom right is held by Archer's Confederates and the bottom left by Lane's. At the top is Gregg's unit, and within two moves of it is Taliaferro's unit. A regiment of Confederate skirmishers drawn from Archer's men is at the bottom of the hill. Union artillery fire precedes Meade's attack; however, due to the open order formation, all Southern casualties are halved. For game purposes, units under artillery fire who take casualties in excess of 5 per cent must move backwards one half of a regular move (not a charge move) and re-form – even before they contact Meade's men. Meade's men may at a walk half move and fire.

Gibbon is held up at the bottom and will not advance unless a '10' is rolled on 1 ten-sided die. Confederate units will be treated as if in open order until they form *after* they have been attacked or have been within 1-inch of a Union unit.

Taliaferro cannot move to aid Gregg's unit until the turn following Gregg's contact with Meade's men. Taliaferro is 18 inches from Gregg at the beginning .

The Union wins if they break through and rout Gregg and Taliaferro. If Meade inflicts more than 40 per cent casualties on both Archer's and Lane's units, Meade wins a minor victory. The Confederates win if they inflict more than 30 per cent casualties on Meade and more than 25 per cent casualties on Gibbon, or if they manage to surround Meade and cut him off from returning to Union lines. If cut off for two turns, Meade's unit surrenders and the Southerners win.

When Meade broke through, Taliaferro moved troops to bolster Gregg's position, and this, along with the lack of Union reinforcements, made Meade's withdrawal and retreat inevitable.

FREDERICKSBURG TODAY

After the defeat at Fredericksburg, Burnside planned an attack in late January over a similar route. Men left winter quarters, such as those they were building here, to march in the infamous and ineffective 'Mud March' toward fords north of Fredericksburg. Lincoln instructed Burnside to turn back and not move troops without notifying him first.

Today Fredericksburg is quiet, returning somewhat to its colonial roots, with a thriving tourist industry and an air of yesterday, with its well kept 1940s facades, one-way streets, historic markers, downtown tourist center, and sleepy river banks. Its grid-like street design, a holdover from early colonial town planning, makes it very difficult to become disoriented or lose one's way. In winter the damp of the river permeates the waterfront buildings, and a chill breeze knifes across Marye's Heights, while a watery winter sun lights but does not warm the land. Such is still the nature of Virginia winter. Little has changed since Lee and Burnside's armies clashed here in December 1862.

Located an hour or more south of Washington, D.C., due south of Quantico Marine base and FBI training center, history-rich Fredericksburg lies one mile west of I-95, five miles east of Chancellorsville, and is bordered by the Wilderness and Spotsylvania Court House battlefields on the west and south. Within minutes by car are Chancellorsville, Aquia Landing, Falmouth, and Chatham mansion, which lies across the river and is open to the public, a gracious old home with flower gardens to the rear and the spires of town visible across the front lawn and the lip of the hill.

Visitors can see all battlefield sites and one or two mansions in a long day and still have time for colonial sightseeing the following day. Tiring of that, a stroll down present-day main street (Caroline Street) yields four or five used book, collectible, and antique stores on each block. Between these lie craft shops, specialty stores, and music shops. Interesting eateries lie on Caroline and within sight along side streets. On the waterfront a colonial era shop in an old warehouse features carriages, carriage rides, period clothing, leather goods, weaponry and metal goods, along with furniture and household goods of the period.

Behind the red brick battlefield visitor center on Marye's Heights is a spacious, shaded parking lot. Another brick building houses a good bookstore and souvenir shop on the Park Service grounds. Like many other structures in town, the red brick makes Fredericksburg look faintly, quaintly, colonial – just as it did in 1861, when some thought it looked a bit Brigadoonish.

A visitor can park downtown, view most of the sites of the riverfront battle, and then drive a mile and a half to the site of the battlefield where the National Park office sits just below the crest of Marye's Heights – now a national cemetery housing the honored dead of several wars. From the cemetery one can look across the crest of the hill, down to the plain where six waves of Union divisions massed, to view the old town and riverbank shrouded in fog which is wispy as a tattered battle flag.

As seen today, the back of the Lacy House (Chatham), Sumner's headquarters during the campaign for Fredericksburg.

Today the stone wall, against which six waves of Union soldiers smashed themselves, has been rebuilt just to the left of the visitor center, at the base of the hill where the cemetery honoring American military men is located.

INDEX

(References to illustrations are shown in **bold**)

Further Reading

Bilby, Joseph G., The Irish Brigade in the Civil War, Combined Publishing, PO Box 307, Conshohocken, NJ 19428 (1998)
Conyngham, D. P., The Irish Brigade and its Campaigns, Fordham University Press, New York (1994)
Crute, Joseph R. Jr., Units of the Confederate States Army, Old Soldier Books, Inc., 18779B N. Frederick Road, Frederick, Md. 20879 (1987)
Guernsey, Alfred H. & Henry M. Alden, Harper's Pictorial History of the Civil War, Gramercy Books, Avenel, NJ (1866)
Henderson, G. F. R., and Jay Luvaas (Ed.), The Civil War: In the Writings of Col. G.F.R. Henderson including, complete, The Campaign of Fredericksburg,
  Da Capo Press, New York (1996)
Hotchkiss, Jed, and Gen. Clement A. Evans (Ed.), Confederate Military History, Vol. III, Virginia, Blue and Gray Press
Katcher, P., The Army of Robert E. Lee, Arms & Armour Press, London (1994)
Long, E. B. and Barbara, The Civil War Day By Day: An Almanac 1861-1865, Doubleday & Company, Garden City, NY (1971)
Marvel, W., The Battle of Fredericksburg, Eastern National Publishers (1993)
Mathless, Paul (Ed.), Voices of the Civil War: Fredericksburg, Time Life Books, Alexandria, Va. (1997)
O'Reilly, Frank A., 'One of the Greatest Military Feats of the War': Military Milestone at Fredericksburg, The Journal of Fredericksburg History, Vol II,
  Historic Fredericksburg Foundation, 604 William Street, Fredericksburg, Va. 22401 (1997)
Palfrey, F. W., Campaigns of the Civil War, Vol. V, The Antietam and Fredericksburg, The Archive Society, 130 Locust Street, Harrisburg, Pa. 17101 (1992)
Savas, Theodore P. And David A. Woodbury, Blood on the Rappahannock: The Battle of Fredericksburg, Essays on Union and Confederate Leadership,
  Regimental Studies Inc., Louisiana State University Press (1995)
Schildt, John W., Stonewall Jackson Day By Day, Antietam Publications, Cherwsville, Maryland (1980)
Scott, Robert N. Bvt. Lt.Col., USA (Ed.), War of the Rebellion: Official Records of the Union and Confederate Armies, Government Printing Office,
  Washington, D.C. (1882)
Stackpole, Edward J., Drama on the Rappahannock: The Fredericksburg Campaign, Bonanza Books, New York (1957)
Tucker, Phillip Thomas (Ed.), The History of the Irish Brigade, Sgt. Kirkland's Museum & Historical Society Inc., 912 Lafayette Blvd., Fredericksburg, Va. (1995)
Warner, Ezra J., Generals in Blue: Lives of the Union Commanders, Louisiana State University Press (1977)
Warner, Ezra J., Generals In Gray: Lives of the Confederate Commanders, Louisiana State University Press (1995)
Whan, Vorin E., Fiasco At Fredericksburg, Pennsylvania State University Press (1961)
Wise, Jennings Cropper, The Long Arm of Lee, Vol.I Bull Run to Fredericksburg, Bison Books, University of Nebraska Press, Lincoln & London (1991)
Wycoff, Mac (Ed.), In Defense of General William B. Franklin at the Battle of Fredericksburg, Virginia, Sgt. Kirkland's Museum & Historical Society,
  912 Lafayette Blvd., Fredericksburg, Va. (1995)